A–Z of
Snake Keeping

A–Z of
Snake Keeping

Chris Mattison

with photographs by the author

 Sterling Publishing Co., Inc.   New York

Published in 1991 by Sterling Publishing Company, Inc.
387 Park Avenue South, New York, N.Y. 10016

ISBN 0-8069-8246-2

First published in the U.K. by Merehurst Press, London.
© 1990 by Chris Mattison
This edition published by arrangement with
Merehurst Press. Available in the United States,
Canada and the Philippine Islands only.
Distributed in Canada by Sterling Publishing
℅ Canadian Manda Group, P.O. Box 920, Station U
Toronto, Ontario, Canada M8Z 5P9

Library of Congress Cataloging-in-Publication Data

Mattison, Christopher.
    A–Z of snake keeping / Chris Mattison; with photographs by the
author.
        p.   cm.
    "First published in the U.K. by Merehurst Press, London. c1990.
    1. Snake culture—Encyclopedias.   2. Snakes—Breeding—
Encyclopedias.   3. Captive snakes—Encyclopedias.   I. Title.
II. Title: A to Z of snake keeping.   III. Title: A–Z of
snake keeping.
SF515.5.S64M37   1991
639.3'96—dc20   90-10178
                                                      CIP

10   9   8   7   6   5   4   3   2   1

AUTHOR'S ACKNOWLEDGMENTS

Not all of the animals which figure in the plates
were owned, collected or bred by me, much as I
would have liked them to be. It is a pleasure to
acknowledge the help of the following persons, who
allowed me to photograph snakes in their collections or provided other assistance:

Bob Applegate, John and Linda Bird, Geoff
Clarke, Cotswold Wildlife Park, Lee Grismer,
Ray Hine, Philip Inzel, Bill Montgomery, Jim
Murphy (Dallas Zoo), Mike Nolan, Nick Nyoka,
Karen Redmond, Charles Sampson/Michelle
Course, Gary Sipperley (San Diego Reptile
Breeders), Terry Thatcher, Luke Yeomans.
Gary Sipperley and Dennis St. John also
allowed me to photograph their reptile housing
and breeding facilities, while Mike Nolan and
Steve Thomas provided various items of
equipment for use in the illustrations.

Apart from the above, numerous people have given
me advice, information and encouragement over the
years; although it is not possible to list them all,
their contributions have been no less important and
no less appreciated.

Line drawings by Gretchen Davison
Editor: Lesley Young
Designer: Carole Perks
Typesetting by Avocet Robinson, Buckingham
Reprographics by J Film Process Ltd, Bangkok,
    Thailand
Printed in Singapore by C.S. Graphics Pte Ltd

CONTENTS

INTRODUCTION

This book contains all the information necessary to maintain and breed the more commonly available species of snakes. The more important sections are those dealing with cages, heating, feeding and hygiene, and these should provide all the information required to make a good start in snake-keeping. The remaining sections give additional information on husbandry and breeding techniques, and brief descriptions of most of the species likely to be of interest to the reader.

Of the 4,000-odd species and subspecies of snakes, only a small proportion make satisfactory captives. The others may be unsuitable because their dietary requirements are hard to cater to, because they are dangerous or because they are rare. There are undoubtedly suitable species which are not regularly available, and some of these may begin to appear in the hobby in the future, but the beginner is well advised to choose from the species listed and, in particular, to gain experience with the more common and easily kept ratsnakes and kingsnakes before becoming too adventurous.

Snakes are, by and large, hardy and undemanding animals – many of them have evolved means of surviving in some of the harshest habitats and conditions on earth. Because of this, they will often cling on to life even though conditions fall far short of their ideal. One of the most difficult aspects of snake-keeping, therefore, is gaining the expertise required to know when things are not right; spotting the subtle differences in behaviour patterns which indicate that the animal is struggling to survive. Only by starting with good, healthy stock and caring for it properly will the beginner learn what is normal behaviour and thus recognise deviations from it. Furthermore, sick snakes are an exception. In over 20 years of snake-keeping I have never needed to take an animal to a veterinarian. Problems are almost invariably caused by one of two factors: purchasing animals which already harbour diseases or parasites, or keeping them in an incorrect environment. The first of these can be avoided by selecting only vigorous, captive-bred stock, the second by studying information in this and other books, based on the experience of people who have made trials and learned from their errors.

For many years, snake-keeping was regarded as a somewhat suspicious occupation carried out by a few rather weird enthusiasts. Most of the animals available were caught from the wild and many were totally unsuitable for confinement, while equipment was borrowed from other hobbies and had to be modified, or was built from scratch. Recent developments, which have increased the availability of suitable animals, equipment and literature, have vastly broadened the appeal of these attractive and interesting animals, and encouraged many more people to involve themselves in the hobby. These people are fortunate in having a firm foundation of expertise to build their interest upon, but happily not everything about snakes is known, nor ever will be – part of the appeal of working with animals is that each one is different and new facts can always be discovered. The only limitation is the amount of time and effort which the hobbyist is prepared to invest.

CHRIS MATTISON
SHEFFIELD, 1990

A

ALBINOS

Albinos are animals in which the normal pigment is absent from the skin, fur, feathers or scales. The blood pigment, haemoglobin, is present, however, and the animal may therefore be pinkish in colour and have pink or red eyes due to the presence of blood vessels. Albinism arises by mutation and has been recorded in many species of snakes. A number of these animals have subsequently been bred from and albino strains now exist for several of the commonly kept species. Other strains consist of 'partial' albinos, in which one or more pigment is absent but some colour remains, e.g. the snake may be white with black eyes. (See also SELECTIVE BREEDING.) (**In colour on page 91**.)

AMELANISTIC SNAKES

Amelanistic animals lack the pigment melanin, which is responsible for black, brown and yellow colours. Amelanistic snakes are therefore pale in colour, although they may have some coloration, especially red or pink, due to the presence of other pigments. Amelanistic strains of many species and subspecies of snakes are available. (**In colour on pages 18 and 119**.)

ANERYTHRISTIC SNAKES

Anerythristic animals lack red pigment, and all red markings are therefore absent. So-called 'black albino' corn snakes are actually anerythristic, having lost all traces of the normal red saddles, while retaining the black borders to them. By combining anerythristic mutations with amelanistic mutations, animals with little or no pigment can be produced (see SELECTIVE BREEDING). (**In colour on page 119.**).

An albino Californian kingsnake (striped phase)

B

BOAS

The family of boas (which also contains the pythons) is certainly the best known to most non-herpetologists, and it is frequently a boa which is responsible for catching the attention of potential snake-keepers. Often, the initial purchase of a common boa is ill-advised, since they usually outgrow the available accommodation, are by no means easy snakes to keep, and are notoriously poor breeders even in the hands of experts. However, this and the other species of boas have a great following and form an interesting and varied family. The pythons are dealt with under a separate heading, but included here are all the species which are commonly classed as 'boas'. They include species from widely separated parts of the world and with an equally wide variety of sizes, shapes, colours and habitat preferences. Several of them are rare in the wild and there is concern over their future, but the species listed here should all be available as captive-bred youngsters, albeit sometimes in very small numbers.

Because of the wide diversity of genera and species within this sub-family, they have been divided into five groups: New World boas; rosy boas; sand boas; Pacific boas; Madagascan boas.

NEW WORLD TROPICAL BOAS

A wide variety of boas are found in South and Central America, mostly from tropical regions. Those that are dealt with here consist of six species in four genera:

☐ *Constrictor constrictor*, the common boa
☐ *Corallus caninus*, the emerald tree boa
☐ *Corallus enhydris*, the Amazon tree boa
☐ *Epicrates cenchria*, the rainbow boa
☐ *Epicrates striatus*, the Haitian boa
☐ *Eunectes notaeus*, the yellow anaconda

Since their treatment differs somewhat, details are given separately for each species.

***Constrictor constrictor* – Common Boa, Boa Constrictor (In colour on pages 19 and 22.)**
The common boa is one of the world's five largest snakes, although its size is often exaggerated. In fact, it rarely exceeds a length of 3 m (10 ft), and reaches breeding size at under 2 m (6½ ft). It is a heavy-bodied species with a basic colour of grey, silver or tan with a series of well-defined dark saddles running down the back. The head is wedge-shaped and there is invariably a dark line passing through the eye and becoming wider towards the angle of the jaw. The tail is short, and tapers sharply from the cloaca.

This species has a huge range over much of South and Central America, and eight different

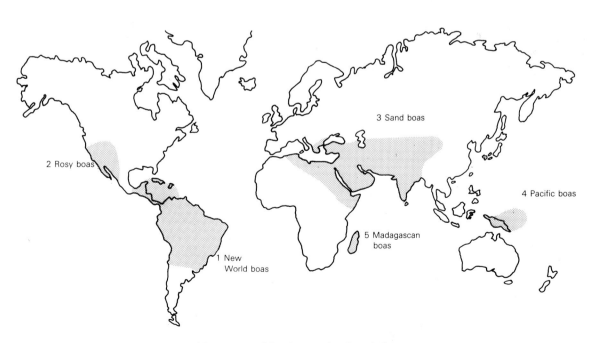

Distribution of the main groupings of boas as used in the species descriptions

Common boa, *Constrictor constrictor*, the species which starts off many snake-keepers

subspecies are recognised. However, there is a great deal of variation even within the subspecies and identification of an individual specimen can be very difficult unless its origin is known. For example, many forms of 'red-tailed' boas exist, but the true red-tailed boa, *C. c. ortoni*, is found only in Peru and is almost never seen in captivity. Other subspecies include a proportion of individuals whose tails are rather more reddish than others and these are often also known as red-tailed boas, although they may originate in the Guianas, Colombia or elsewhere. They are all attractive.

Two other distinctive forms are the Argentine boa, *C. c. occidentalis*, which has a network of intricate black or chocolate-brown markings over a silver background, and the so-called 'Hog Island boa', from the Honduras region, which is grey in colour, peppered with tiny dark spots, and often has a number of pink scales arranged in irregular patches. This boa remains smaller than the other forms, and its colour may change from light to dark according to conditions.

There are also other forms of common boa which are not nearly as attractive as any of the above. These tend to be nondescript brownish snakes with indistinct saddles and blotches along their backs.

Care of the common boa, in all its forms, centres around the use of a suitable cage. Young animals can be accommodated in much the same way as the larger colubrids, i.e. in boxes or small glass-fronted cages, but adults require almost room-sized pens. They are semi-arboreal and should be given the opportunity to climb up a stout branch. Many will use a shelf, raised off the floor of the cage, to bask in an overhead heat source such as a ceramic heater. A temperature of about 28°C (82°F) should be provided, with one area giving slightly more than this and another giving slightly less – in other words, a somewhat 'compressed' thermal gradient (see HEATING).

A large water bowl is important since this species likes to soak, and common sense dictates that this should be kept only half full or less, otherwise it will flood when the snake submerges itself. Substrate on the floor of the cage may be newspaper, wood shavings or one of the more modern materials such as pellets

of compressed sawdust, clean bark chippings or corn husks.

Food consists of rodents or birds. Young boa constrictors will usually readily accept mice and move on to rats as they grow, although some seem to prefer chicks. Adults are more economically fed on rabbits or chickens.

Breeding techniques appear to be something of a mystery and there is no sure way of inducing these snakes to breed. It is probable

The emerald tree boa, *Corallus canina*, resting in its characteristic posture

that a drop in temperature, to about 20-22°C (68-72°F), during the winter is important, and it may be beneficial to increase the humidity slightly at this time. It is important that the breeders, especially the females, are in good condition; the female will often fast for almost the entire six months or so while pregnant. However, overfed animals are reluctant to breed, and activity and exercise may be an important element in keeping this species in good breeding condition. Litters of up to 50 young have been recorded, although young adults may produce less than ten. These vary in size from 35-60 cm (14-24 in), but are usually capable of taking half-grown to adult mice readily.

Corallus caninus – Emerald Tree Boa
(In colour on page 23.)

Undoubtedly the most brilliant of the boas, this arboreal species is bright green in colour, usually with irregular white markings arranged along the centre of the back. Some individuals lack these dorsal markings, however, and are plain green. This snake invariably drapes itself over a horizontal branch with its head resting in the centre of its coils, and rarely comes down to the ground. Large heat-sensitive pits are situated between the scales bordering the upper jaw.

The juveniles are totally different, being bright sulphur-yellow, or brick-red. Only the white dorsal markings, if present, remain unchanged throughout the life of the snake.

Emerald tree boas require a tall vivarium, for instance, a 50 × 50 cm (20 × 20 in) base and a height of 75 cm (30 in), equipped with a branch or stout dowel, fixed firmly across the cage about two-thirds of the way up. Substrate may be newspaper, bark chippings or wood shavings, etc. A temperature of 28-30°C (82-86°F) is required at all times, slightly more

for pregnant females, which like to bask beneath a heat source. The cage should be sprayed regularly to provide a moderately high humidity. Food consists of mice and rats, which are most easily offered to the snake using long feeding forceps. Some individuals prefer birds such as quail and chicks.

Breeding takes place in response to an increase in humidity. At this time the ventilation to the cage should be covered for a few hours immediately after spraying. Small litters, of up to 15 young, are born after a gestation period of about six months, but much patience is often needed before the young can be induced to feed, and they sometimes require lizards at first.

Corallus enhydris – **Amazon Tree Boa**

This South American boa grows to about 150 cm (5 ft) and is similar in form to the emerald tree boa but rather more slender. It is easily the most variable species of boa, and hardly any two snakes look the same! Two subspecies, *C. e. enhydris* and *C. e. cooki* are recognised, but the variation between individuals makes a description of these superfluous. The background colour may be yellow, tan, red, dark green or brown and markings may or may not be present. If they are, they can consist of bars, circles or rhomboids of darker or lighter colour! A single litter of young can contain a whole spectrum of types.

Care and breeding are roughly similar to that of the emerald tree boa, but this species is rather more active (and aggressive!). Its cage should be tall (although this species will come down to the ground sometimes), and should contain a number of branches around which the boa will wrap itself. A temperature of about 30°C (86°F) is required, but this may be allowed to fall to about 25°C (77°F) during the winter. Mating will then take place in the spring, with the young being born 200-250 days later. Litters number up to 20 in size. Although the young may accept relatively large mice, some require lizards or force-feeding at first.

Notes: a third species, *Corallus annulatus*, also exists but is rarely available. *Corallus hortulanus* is an older name for *C. enhydris*.

Epicrates cenchria – **Rainbow Boa**
(In colour on page 19.)

The rainbow boa grows to almost 2 m (6½ ft) and has a large range over much of South America. About eight subspecies are recognised, of which three are sometimes available. Basic coloration is of brown, tan or orange with circles of black down the back and additional smaller circles along the flanks – these may have light centres. The most colourful subspecies is the Brazilian rainbow boa, *E. cenchria cenchria*, which has a rich reddish-brown or orange background with distinct markings. The 'Colombian' rainbow boa (its range actually extends much further than Colombia), *E. c. maurus*, is browner in colour and the markings become less distinct with age. The Argentinian rainbow boa, *E. c. alvarezi*, is distinctly different from the others in that the areas around the rings are darker than their pale brown or beige centres, giving a more reticulated pattern.

The Amazon tree boa, *Corallus enhydris*, comes in a variety of forms. This example is pale yellow in colour

Care of all these subspecies is similar. They are somewhat less demanding than the common boa but require similar accommodation, temperature and food. Their breeding habits are more predictable: the temperature should be allowed to fall to about 20-22°C (68-72°F) in the winter and they will then mate during the spring. Litters of up to 20 young are born after a gestation of about 200 days. The babies are more brightly marked than the adults and usually feed readily on young mice.

Epicrates striatus – Haitian Boa

This species grows rather longer than the rainbow boa but is more slender in build. It is heavily blotched in dark reddish-brown over a paler background and there are numerous irregular dark markings on the flanks. Its temperament is less amenable than the rainbow boa, and this species makes an altogether less suitable captive.

An unusual small Central American boa, *Ungaliophis continentalis*

It requires a fairly tall cage with branches, since it likes to climb occasionally. Temperature and food are as for the rainbow boa. Adults will mate in the spring after a period of cooling down, and the litters, consisting of about ten young, are born about six months later. Babies sometimes eat newborn mice, but often need to be tempted with lizards or fish at first. They can sometimes be induced to feed by placing them in a small container with their food.

Note: seven other species of *Epicrates* are found on various West Indian islands: several of these are in danger of extinction due to the fragile state of the ecology on their respective islands. In general, none of them make good captives: those that are not fully protected by law are smaller, more slender species which appear to eat mainly lizards, especially when young.

Eunectes notaeus – Yellow Anaconda

The yellow anaconda is yellowish-brown in colour with darker blotches along the back and flanks. It is a heavy-bodied species which, in the wild, spends most of its time in a semi-aquatic situation. Growing to a maximum of 3 m (10 ft),

Yellow anaconda, *Eunectes notaeus*

this species is somewhat smaller than its more illustrious relative, *Eunectes murinus*, the green anaconda, but is still an ambitious undertaking for the amateur snake-keeper. Its temperament often leaves a lot to be desired and as it grows its markings become less distinct and colourful.

Mating takes place after a period of slight cooling down and the litters of up to 20 young are born after a gestation of eight to nine months. They are a good size when born and will usually accept half-grown mice straightaway: any which do not can usually be induced to feed on fish.

Notes: the green anaconda, *Eunectes murinus*, is the largest snake in the world. It is also one of the most bad tempered and is therefore unsuitable for private collections unless these are equipped with the necessary space and facilities for such a gigantic reptile.

In addition, two other genera, *Tropidophis*, with twelve species in the West Indies, and *Ungaliophis*, with two species in Central America, are very occasionally available, while two rare genera are almost never seen. All of these are small boas, which can be accommodated much as for tropical colubrids, but captive breeding is uncommon.

THE ROSY BOAS (In colour on page 26.)

The rosy boas comprise a single species, *Lichanura trivirgata*, with probably four distinct subspecies. Local geographical variation makes their classification difficult and this is somewhat chaotic at present, with two systems in use. A general description of the species is as follows. The body is cylindrical and the head very small. The maximum size appears to be about 1 m (3 ft), although most individuals are somewhat smaller than this. The scales are small and smooth so that the surface has a lustrous appearance, and there are no heat-sensitive pits. Background coloration may be brown or cream with a tendency for stripes in certain forms. Subspecies are as follows:

The Mexican subspecies of the rosy boa, *Lichanura t. trivirgata*, has chocolate-brown and cream stripes

Lichanura trivirgata trivirgata, the Mexican rosy boa, occurs on the mainland of Mexico in the state of Sinaloa and in the southern portion of Baja California. It is pale cream in colour with three bold stripes of deep chocolate-brown running the length of the body, one along the back and one on each flank.

Lichanura trivirgata gracia, the desert rosy boa, is found in Arizona and in adjacent desert regions of California. It is cream or pale grey in colour with ragged stripes of orange running the length of its body.

Lichanura trivirgata roseofusca, the coastal rosy boa, is found in southern California and northern Baja California. It may be a uniform brown in colour or there may be signs of three irregular slate-grey stripes running along the body. Confusingly, examples from the desert portions of the range are more distinctly striped, i.e. they tend towards the coloration of the desert rosy boa, *L. t. gracia*.

Lichanura trivirgata (myriolepis), the Central Baja rosy boa, is found in the central region of Baja California. This subspecies is similar to *L. t. gracia* but the edges of the stripes are generally more even.

If recent revisions are accepted the names will change as follows: *L. t. trivirgata* will remain the same. *L. t. gracia* will become *L. t. myriolepis* and this subspecies will also include most of the specimens presently included in *L. t. roseofusca*. *L. t. roseofusca* will be included in *L. t. myriolepis*, except for a small population of uniform brown snakes centred around the southern California/Baja California border, which will remain as *L. t. roseofusca*. *L. t. myriolepis* will become *L. t. saslowi*. An additional subspecies, *L. t. bosticki* is recognised from the island of Cedros, off the Pacific coast of Baja California.

Fortunately, all these subspecies, irrespective of their names, can be cared for in the same way. Although not as easy as kingsnakes, for instance, rosy boas should be treated in a similar manner to colubrids from the same part of the world. They may be housed in boxes, cages with drawers or modified aquaria, etc., and given a thermal gradient. Despite their mainly desert origins, many of them like to climb and a branch is a useful, though not essential, addition. The substrate may be of newspaper, wood shavings, etc. and should be kept dry. Most rosy boas feed readily on small

Albinos

Amelanistic black ratsnake, *Elaphe obsoleta*. All black pigment (melanin) is missing, so the markings consist of only of the underlying red pigments

Amelanistic prairie kingsnake, *Lampropeltis c. calligaster*

South and Central American Boas (1)

Common boa, *Constrictor constrictor*

The brightly coloured Brazilian subspecies of the rainbow boa, *Epicrates cenchria cenchria*

mice. Some refuse anything larger than a slightly furred mouse for the whole of their lives but others will happily take adult mice. There is a great deal of individual variation in their willingness to feed and in the amount of food taken.

Breeding is fairly straightforward: the adults are cooled down to about 12-15°C (54-59°F) in the winter and will mate when they are warmed up in the spring. The gestation period is just over 100 days and females may refuse to feed towards the end of this period. Small litters of up to six young are born and these are about 25-30 cm (10-12 in) in length. Most will feed readily on newborn mice, although there may be a long period of fasting before the first meal is taken. Occasional young will refuse to feed voluntarily and must be force-fed for a while.

Eryx jaculus, a small sand boa which is the only member of the boa family to be found in Europe

SAND BOAS

The sand boas form a distinct grouping of ten species which are African and Asian in origin (although one species just about reaches south-eastern Europe). They are small, but heavily built snakes with very short tails and small heads. Their natural inclination is to burrow and this should be catered to in captivity. They are conveniently kept in plastic boxes with a layer of fine sand or wood shavings covering the bottom to a depth of about 5 cm (2 in). Drinking water should be available. A temperature of about 23-27°C (73-81°F) seems to suit all species, but there should be opportunities to thermoregulate, achieved by heating one end of the container only. Most will take mice readily, but the young of some species are sometimes more willing to feed on lizards. Breeding is stimulated by reducing the

temperature in the winter, as for colubrids. Only a few species are freely available, and they are rarely bred in captivity, being of more interest to the specialist snake-keeper.

Eryx colubrinus – Kenyan or Egyptian Sand Boa (In colour on page 26.)

This African species is pale brown, tan or yellowish in colour with darker brown blotches along the back and flanks. The subspecies *E. c. loveridgei*, from Kenya, is the most attractive form, with chocolate-brown blotches on an orange or yellow background. Litters of 5–15 young are born after a gestation of six to seven months. They measure about 15 cm and will normally feed on newborn mice.

Eryx conicus – Rough-scaled Sand Boa

This species comes from Pakistan and India and is similar to the above species in appearance, except that the colours are more muted and the scales are heavily keeled. Its care and breeding are exactly the same, and litters comprise up to ten young, each measuring about 20 cm (8 in) in length.

Eryx johnii – Smooth-scaled Sand Boa

This is a plain brown sand boa from India and Pakistan. It grows rather larger than the other species and may reach 1 m (3 ft) or more. It has a blunt tail and if disturbed it may raise this in the air as a false head while the real head is hidden in the coils. It is very docile in captivity and usually feeds well.

Care and breeding are as for the other species of *Eryx*. From 5-15 young are born and these measure about 25 cm (10 in) in length. They are lightly banded at birth, and usually take newborn mice without any problems.

Note: certain of the other seven species of *Eryx* may occasionally appear on the market. Their care should be similar to that described above.

GROUP 4

PACIFIC BOAS

A group of three boas belonging to the genus *Candoia* are found on the Pacific islands of New Guinea, the Solomon Islands, the New Hebrides and neighbouring groups. These interesting species are small to medium in size and make good captives under the right conditions. Only one of the three is readily available, while a second crops up from time to time. The third species is only rarely seen.

Candoia aspera – Pacific Ground Boa (In colour on page 26.)

The smallest of the group, *C. aspera* grows to about 75 cm (30 in). It is extremely heavy-bodied and has a distinctive angled snout. The scales are heavily keeled and the colour is brown with obscure dark brown markings. Young snakes may be reddish-brown in colour.

This species requires a small box with a substrate of bark chippings. It comes from a humid environment and seems to benefit from an occasional spraying: some individuals will refuse to feed unless the humidity is maintained at a high level. A temperature of 25-30°C (77-86°F) is required. It is rarely bred in captivity, but young born to wild-caught females have been small and are difficult to persuade to start feeding.

Candoia carinata – Pacific Boa

This species may eventually grow to about 1.5 m (5 ft) and adults are almost as thick-bodied as the preceding species. However, it is easily distinguished by its smoother scales and more distinct markings. These consist of a dark stripe running down the back – this line sprouts short alternating branches along its length to give an almost zig-zag pattern. The most common coloration is of a brick-red stripe on a paler background, but some individuals (perhaps from a different chain of islands) are pale grey or cream with a reddish-edged ash-grey stripe. It is sometimes known by the name 'viper boa'.

It requires a medium-sized cage and should be kept dry, unlike the previous species. Adults feed readily on mice. They need a temperature of about 25-30°C (77-86°F), but this should be reduced to about 20°C (68°F) in the winter if it is hoped to breed them. They have large litters of up to 65 young, but these are very small – about 20-25 cm (8-10 in) in length, and thin. Some of the young will take newborn mice, but others can be a problem and may require force-feeding at first unless small lizards are available.

Note: the third species, *Candoia bibronii*, is more slender than the other two species and is arboreal in habit. Its vertebral stripe is even more viper-like. It is only rarely seen, usually being imported by accident with *C. carinata*, and has probably not been bred in captivity.

South and Central American Boas (2)

The Hog Island boa, *Constrictor contrictor* subsp., is smaller than typical common boas and is paler in colour. It also has a limited ability to change colour

Emerald tree boa, *Corallus canina*. Note that the heat-sensitive pits are located between the scales

MADAGASCAN BOAS

The island of Madagascar is home to three species of boas. Of these, only one is regularly bred in captivity.

Acrantophis dumerilii – Dumeril's Boa

Dumeril's boa is listed as an endangered species and is placed on Appendix I of CITES (see LAWS). This means that an exemption must be obtained before it can be kept in captivity. However, it is bred in fairly large numbers.

It grows to about 2 m (6½ ft) in length and is pale yellowish-brown in colour with a complicated arrangement of darker markings. These are interconnected and form an irregular dark reticulation over the whole of the body. There may be pinkish or red areas on the head and neck, especially in young snakes.

This species requires a large cage with a temperature of about 25-30°C (77-86°F), which should be reduced by about 5°C (9°F) in winter in order to induce breeding. The food is rodents and should not present any problems, although some individuals seem to prefer birds such as quail. Litters consist of two to six large young, measuring up to 70 cm (28 in) in length. Rearing these is usually straightforward.

Notes: the other species in the genus is *Acrantophis madagascariensis*, the Madagascan ground boa, which has similar requirements although it attains a larger size. *Sanzinia madagascariensis* is the Madagascan tree boa, which may be treated in much the same way as the South American arboreal species such as *Corallus enhydris*, although this snake is not as easy to keep or breed. Both these Madagascan species are listed on Appendix I of CITES and are practically unobtainable through legal channels.

BREEDING

Breeding should be the aim of all responsible snake-keepers. The capture of snakes from the wild has had serious effects on natural populations and, in some cases, on their habitats (although in most cases this has been negligible compared to the habitat destruction caused by agriculture, logging and industrial development). Now that the techniques for inducing snakes to breed are well known there should be no need to draw on wild populations except to introduce new species to the hobby or to help to prevent inbreeding by obtaining the odd wild individual which is unrelated to existing breeding stocks.

It is important to remember that snakes are driven by the same urge to reproduce as every other living organism: it is not necessary to 'make' them breed, just to 'let' them breed! Doing this successfully is accomplished by paying attention to such basic factors as their environment and feeding, coupled with some knowledge of the more specialised techniques described under the headings SEX DETERMINATION, EGG-LAYING or LIVE-BEARING, INCUBATING EGGS and HATCHLINGS.

Snakes from which it is hoped to breed also require a certain amount of pre-conditioning. In its simplest form this means that they should be well fed (but not overfed), and free from diseases and parasites. Wild-caught snakes can take up to two years to settle into a captive environment and they cannot be expected to breed successfully until this has occurred. Wherever possible, a breeding pair of snakes should be well matched for size and should be of the same genetic type (see HYBRIDS and SELECTIVE BREEDING). They should be housed separately except when they are paired up, and then left together until copulation has been observed several times or until the female is obviously forming eggs.

North American and European snakes almost always require a cooling down period before they will produce fertile eggs. This is because the males cannot produce viable sperm at high temperatures and even if they mate the resulting eggs will be infertile. Generally speaking, temperatures of about 15°C (59°F) should be aimed for, but some montane species require even lower temperatures (see HIBERNATION). Mating will then take place in the spring, almost as soon as the animals are warmed up. Tropical species also need to be cooled down, although possibly not so drastically. Note that some species mate at this time of year and so should be put together while they are cool. More detailed information is provided for individual species in the sections in which they are described.

BUYING SNAKES

Careful selection of the snake, the species and the dealer or breeder from whom it is purchased are the first steps towards successfully keeping and breeding snakes. Buying any item of livestock is not like buying a book or a freezer. For a start, all animals are individuals and no two are exactly alike in their appearance or behaviour. In addition to this, once a snake is purchased, its fate is, to a large extent, dependent on the knowledge and skill of the purchaser, and so very few dealers will guarantee that their animals will survive for longer than a few days, given the fact that they have no control over the way in which they are treated.

For these reasons, it is vitally important to make sure that the snakes which are purchased are in good condition and *exactly* as required, especially with regard to their sex. Any good dealer will value his reputation and be happy to allow prospective customers to inspect the stock personally (within reason) and will reassure them that the animals are correctly sexed.

Regarding the choice of species, no snake should be bought until its requirements regarding food, accommodation, etc. are properly researched and it is known that they can be properly met. If young snakes are purchased it is important to know how big they will eventually grow. If the species concerned grows too large, do not buy it. Snakes cannot be stunted or kept small like bonsai trees and there is very little market for 20-ft pythons which have outgrown their cage, taken over the house and eaten the children!

Having selected a suitable species, all individual animals purchased should be free from external injuries, disease or parasites (as far as it is possible to see). In the case of captive-bred hatchlings it is often advantageous if the parents can also be inspected, since in many species the colours and markings of juveniles will change as they grow. This is especially important with species which show great variation in their pattern and coloration.

If the intention is to breed snakes, try to obtain a male and a female at the same time. Breeders are understandably reluctant to part with odd animals, especially females, and many people search in vain for a mate for the three-year old snake which they bought as a singleton in the hope that they could pair it up later. When buying a pair of snakes from a breeder, he or she should guarantee that the sexes are correct, but nobody is infallible and it is always as well to check this straightaway (see SEX DETERMINATION), because there will be very little the breeder can do to put matters right months later when all his or her surplus stock will almost certainly have been sold. If one breeder cannot offer unrelated offspring and there is some concern over the possibility of inbreeding depression (e.g. if brothers have been mated with sisters for three or more generations), it may be necessary to buy one pair of snakes from one breeder and one pair from another (assuming that their stocks are unrelated) and then mate the male of one pair with the female of the other, and vice versa. If two pairs are more than are required, find another snake-keeper who is interested in the same species and come to an arrangement whereby each of you takes an unrelated pair.

Small Boas

Coastal rosy boa, *Licahnura trivirgata roseofusca*

Kenyan sand boa, *Eryx colubrinus loveridgei.* This subspecies is almost certainly the most colourful member of its genus

The Pacific ground boa, *Candoia aspera*, is an interesting but rarely seen species

Garter Snakes

The chequered garter snake, *Thamnophis marcianus*, is one of the toughest garter snakes

The Florida subspecies of the common garter snake, *Thamnophis sirtalis similis*

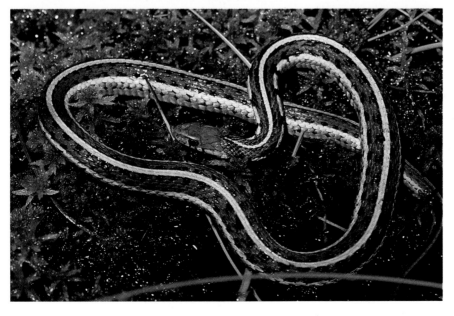

Eastern garter snake, *Thamnophis sirtalis sirtalis*

C

CAGES

Cages suitable for housing snakes can rarely be bought ready-made, therefore a certain amount of improvisation is necessary. This can take two forms: self-built cages constructed to a design appropriate to the species being kept, perhaps with some modifications to suit individual budgets and requirements; or the adaptation of containers made and sold for other purposes.

The three essential requirements of any cage are that it should be: escape-proof; capable of producing the correct environment; easy to clean. The ultimate design depends heavily on (i) the kind and size of snake which is to be accommodated, and (ii) whether the cage is to be used to display the snake or merely to house and breed from it. Either way, there is no one standard type which can be recommended, but alternatives can be suggested which should cover practically any situation.

Cages for large snakes

Snakes of 1.8 m (6 ft) or more in length, such as the larger boas and pythons, require spacious cages constructed from sturdy materials. A good starting point is a wooden-bodied cabinet with a sliding glass front. The inside of the cage should be varnished, painted with gloss paint or, better still, plastic laminated. The front should comprise two glass panels which slide back on one another, slotted into a double channel of the correct width. The edges of the glass should be ground in order to allow them to slide easily and to prevent injury. They can be secured in place when closed with small rubber or wood wedges or by using the type of locks used in shop showcases. Unless

A showcase lock, useful for extra security on cages with sliding glass, and essential where venomous species are housed

newspaper is to be used as bedding it is useful if the bottom channel holding the glass is raised an inch or two on a wooden lip. This will prevent the bedding from falling out all over the floor every time the glass is slid back! The floor should be well supported along its length to prevent the weight of the snake, water bowl, etc. from causing it to sag, resulting in difficulty in sliding the glass, or worse, gaps forming. Ventilation for this type of cage takes the form of one or more panels of perforated metal or plastic, or metal gauze, securely fixed into the back or sides.

If several large snakes are to be housed in the same room, a unit consisting of the required

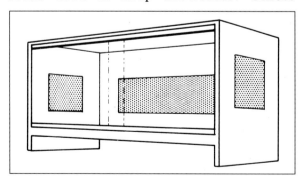

A simple snake cage with a sliding glass front and a ventilation panel in the back. The construction is of plastic-faced timber

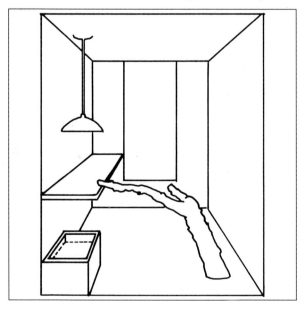

Plan of a walk-in python or boa cage, with a shelf for basking, a stout bough and a large water container

A large walk-in cage, suitable for housing a breeding group of pythons, built by Dennis St John, California

A purpose-built snake room, equipped with several large walk-in cages

number of such cages is easily designed, but care must be taken to ensure that each has adequate ventilation.

Serious breeders of large snakes often construct walk-in cages. These are built into part of a snake room, using wooden or brick walls. The floor should be sealed and there should be a step-up lip across the bottom of the doorway. The door should open outwards or slide back along the outside of the compartment to prevent possible injury to the snake(s). Many large snakes appreciate a sturdy shelf built along one wall, on which they will coil for much of the time. If overhead heating is used (see HEATING) this should be suspended above the shelf so that the snake can bask on the shelf or crawl beneath it if it needs to cool down.

Cages for medium-sized snakes

The majority of snakes kept in captivity are within the range of 1-2 m (3-6½ ft) in length. These snakes may be housed in a variety of cages. The sliding glass cabinet type described above can be scaled down, and several can be built into a single unit, creating condominium or high-rise accommodation. If necessary, the glass front of each 'apartment' can consist of a single panel, sliding up or to one side to provide access. Alternatively, the front can consist of a hinged wooden frame containing a panel of glass, like the door of a cupboard.

A refinement to this design is to incorporate a shallow drawer beneath the main section, with a short piece of plastic tubing linking the two compartments. Many species of snakes like to be able to spend time 'underground' and this system caters well for them. By placing a plug in the connecting pipe, the cage can be temporarily divided into two sections, which is a convenient way of separating the snakes during feeding, etc. Those of us who lack the skill to construct a well-fitting drawer can make use of ready-made plastic trays such as cat-litter trays, seed trays or washing-up bowls, and design the upper portion in such a way that the

Gopher Snakes and Relatives

Arizona elegans pacata, a subspecies of glossy snake which is found in Baja California

The Sonoran gopher snake, *Pituophis melanoleucus affinis*, is one of the smaller members of its genus and is often better tempered than some of the others

Northern pine snake, *Pituophis melanoleucus melanoleucus*

Green Snake

The rough green snake,
Opheodryas aestivus, an
attractive insectivorous
snake which is suitable
for a naturally arranged
vivarium

Rough green snake,
Opheodryas aestivus

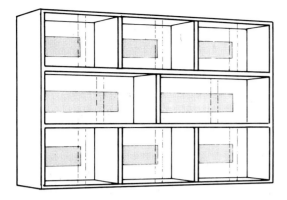

A unit consisting of eight snake cages with sliding glass fronts

item of choice is a snug fit. The additional benefits of this arrangement are that the trays can easily be cleaned and sterilised, and that a few extra trays can be kept to one side and used as quick replacements during cleaning operations.

Modified aquaria may be used as snake cages, but are not ideal in the long term. They are useful for quarantining animals or for displaying them temporarily, but should be thoughtfully adapted so that the lid provides ventilation and can be thoroughly secured. There is at least one excellent cage of this design on the market, which is fitted with a perforated stainless steel lid which slides into place and can be secured with a pin or a padlock.

Snakes placed on display may be housed in cages which are specially constructed. These

can be based on any of the designs suggested above, or may be made for a particular purpose. Often, these cages are a compromise between appearance and convenience, and some ease of servicing may be sacrificed, but it must be possible to clean them thoroughly when necessary. Their shape and size can be made to suit the habits of the species to be contained. It is often possible to enclose some living plants as well as rocks and branches in order to provide a reasonable simulation of the snake's natural habitat.

At the other extreme, snakes which are not on display can be kept very easily and successfully in plastic- or polyethylene food containers. Adults of the smaller species, such as several of the milksnakes, hognose snakes and so on, will live their whole lives in boxes measuring about 40 × 40 cm (16 × 16 in). Panels of fine wire gauze should be fixed into the lid or sides (or both), and the boxes placed on a heating pad or cable. The advantage of this type of accommodation is that it is cheap, easily cleaned and disinfected and the snakes like the security of living in a relatively small area (provided that they are not of the more active species). By using a specially constructed rack to hold the boxes (see below) a large number can be kept in a limited amount of space and heated very cheaply.

Cages for small snakes, including hatchlings
Small species of snakes, and juveniles of the larger species, are most easily accommodated in small lunch- or shoe-boxes. These must be ventilated by fitting a panel of wire gauze, or by drilling a series of holes in one end (which becomes the front). Most boxes of this type do not have tightly fitting lids and so, if a small number are used, some type of clip must be devised to prevent the snakes from escaping. On the other hand, if a reasonable quantity are used, for instance to accommodate the offspring from a successful breeding season, these should be kept in a rack system, in which case the lids are kept in place by the shelf above that on which they are resting (assuming, of course, that the shelves are spaced accurately). Heating of the boxes is also easily and cheaply achieved using this system (see HEATING).

A bank of cages with false bottoms and a drawer, used to house colubrids and small boas or pythons. This unit, and those in the next three photographs, was built by Gary Sipperley (San Diego Reptile Breeders)

A rack holding shoe-boxes or lunch-boxes for housing small snakes. Unless the boxes are an accurate fit between the shelves, as here, or the lid is of a snap-on type, a clip or band must be used to prevent the snake from pushing the lid off

Construction of the rack itself is not too difficult, even for persons with limited ability in the woodworking department. The diagram should be self-explanatory, but points to note are that the shelves should be rebated if heat tape or heat cable is used, and that some provision should be made to replace the heat tape or cable should it be necessary. One way of doing this is to notch out the side pieces (ends) of the rack, but an even simpler method is simply to allow the shelves to project the required amount at the back. Additional information is given under HEATING.

Larger snakes can also be accommodated in plastic boxes. Here, the cages fit so well between the shelves that a lid is unnecessary. This calls for considerable woodworking skill!

The drawer of this cage has been opened to show the 'basement' living area

A small plastic food container, suitable for housing hatchling kingsnakes, ratsnakes, etc., complete with bedding, a water bowl and a snake (prairie kingsnake)

Cage furnishings

Snake cages should be kept as simple as possible. This prevents parasites from hiding in cracks and crevices and makes cleaning and servicing easier. It seems pretty safe to assume that snakes have no aesthetic appreciation, and so any artistic efforts on the part of their keeper will be solely for his or her benefit.

The most widely used types of bedding are newspaper, cut to size and laid on the floor of the cage, or soft wood shavings. Slightly more attractive, and almost as practical, but only for small snakes, are the small clay beads sold for horticultural purposes. These should be washed before use to get rid of dust, and can be rewashed and dried out as necessary. Other types of bedding that have been used with varying degrees of success include bark chippings (which tend to be very dusty) and pea-gravel (which tends to harbour parasites). Dry dead leaves, pine needles and bracken, etc. can be used in conjunction with newspaper to give a more natural appearance to the cage or to illustrate aspects of biology such as camouflage, but they should be changed regularly.

Other than bedding, the most essential item is a water bowl. This can be of practically any type so long as it can be washed out and disinfected occasionally. Plastic or glazed earthenware are probably the best materials.

A variety of substrates may be used in snake cages, including wood shavings, pumice, bark chippings and clay beads. The main requirement is that the material is dry and can be washed or changed easily.

Precautions against spillage should be taken, as a permanently damp substrate in the cage will lead to all sorts of health problems. Heavy water bowls are therefore preferable to light plastic ones, but plastic tubs with access holes cut into the lids are difficult for the snakes to overturn, and will not spill when tipped onto their sides. In addition, wood shavings are less likely to find their way into the bowl. Also, many snakes like to soak, especially when they are about to shed their skins, and this type of water bowl allows them to crawl inside and soak without feeling exposed. In this way they double as a water bowl and hide-box.

Hide-boxes may also be included in the cage as a separate item. In the wild snakes spend most of their time coiled up under a rock or in a narrow crevice, and if they are unable to get most of their body in contact with something solid they will suffer from stress. Although snakes in small cages, such as the lunch- and shoe-boxes mentioned above, will enjoy the security which comes with living in a confined space, larger cages must contain a smaller compartment where the snake can hide. If a drawer is part of the design then this will serve the purpose admirably, but otherwise a wooden or plastic box with a small opening should be placed inside the cage. The snake will spend much of its time in here, behaving as it would in the wild, and may also prefer to be fed in its hide-box. If the entrance to the hide-box can be closed, by a slide or some sort of plug, then it can be lifted out, complete with snake, during cleaning, and this will help to prevent unnecessary handling. Snakes which have the security of a hide-box settle in more quickly, feed better and eventually become tamer than those which are forced out into the open by being housed in a large bare cage.

Other items are largely a matter of choice and will do little to increase the lifespan or contentment of the snake. Having said this, if cages are attractively set up, the interest of the keeper is more likely to be maintained and this obviously leads to a more conscientious approach to husbandry. The design and decoration of a display cage must be carefully thought out. Perhaps more important, the choice of suitable species is very limited and there is no future in trying to simulate swamps for garter snakes or tropical rain forests for boa constrictors. However, some suggestions for displaying certain snakes in an attractive and educational manner are given.

The use of inert substances, e.g. clay beads, is recommended for the bedding. Branches and rocks should be kept to a minimum and plants should either be epiphytes, such as orchids and bromeliads, which can be attached to branches, or they should be kept in pots, with a layer of clay beads or pebbles on the surface to prevent the snakes from redistributing the soil or compost all over the cage. Lighting, which is of little importance to the snake itself, will be necessary for the plants to thrive, but there must be ample opportunity for the snake to find a secluded place to hide away. A number of fluorescent tubes are available which have been developed for the horticultural industry, and one or more of these will improve the health and appearance of any living plant material.

Unfortunately, maintaining a natural or semi-natural cage for large snakes is not practicable as they are powerful animals which rapidly cancel out any efforts to landscape their cage. Slender tree snakes are a good choice for this type of treatment, although there are few suitable species to choose from (most tree snakes are lizard- or frog-eaters). The North American green snakes (*Opheodryas*), are ideally suited to a well-decorated cage, however, although if they are fed on crickets any uneaten food may, in turn, make a meal out of the plants. Small desert snakes, such as the shovel-nosed snakes and sand snakes (*Chionactis* and *Chilomeniscus*) are difficult to maintain unless some concession is made to their lifestyle, since they have specialised habits. Here, a layer of horticultural sand is necessary for the snakes to burrow into, and the set-up can be enhanced by the inclusion of some pieces of dead wood (cactus skeletons are very suitable) and even one or two succulent plants with their pots plunged into the sand.

CAPTIVE-BRED SNAKES

Many species of snakes are now being bred in captivity, especially in the United States but, increasingly, also in Europe. This trend began in the 1970s when it was realised that many species were becoming rare in the wild and they were therefore legally protected. Amateur snake-keepers began to experiment with the conditions under which they kept their animals until, eventually, the requirements necessary to induce them to breed became better understood. At present, a number of people make a reasonable living entirely from breeding snakes and many more supplement their income by breeding snakes in their spare time. The outcome of this activity is that most of the more desirable species of snakes are now available without the necessity to deplete wild stocks, except for occasional additions of fresh animals which are necessary to prevent inbreeding.

A further aspect of this trend is the appearance of several unusual strains of snakes, having arisen either as mutations from breeding stock, or descending from a wild mutant individual. These include albinos, animals lacking one or more of their normal pigments, or animals with markings which differ in some other respect from their wild ancestors. This has enabled selective breeding to take place and, although opinions vary as to whether or not some of these strains are more attractive than normal ones, they have added greatly to the variety of snakes which are available to the snake-keeper.

Captive-bred snakes have several other advantages over wild-caught ones:

☐ They are more likely to be free from disease or parasites.

☐ They are more likely to adapt quickly and successfully to captivity.

☐ Many species which are rare in the wild, and therefore formerly expensive, are now available at very reasonable prices due to the fact that they are bred in large numbers.

☐ The breeder or supplier will usually be able to guarantee their sexes, and may be able to supply unrelated young.

☐ They will have the maximum amount of their life-span in front of them.

The species which are bred in the largest numbers come from North and Central America and belong to the family Colubridae, i.e. they are colubrids, and are harmless. All the species which are readily available as captive-bred hatchlings are dealt with under the appropriate headings in this book. Special requirements for captive-bred hatchlings are described under HATCHLINGS and FEEDING HATCHLINGS.

Captive breeding and conservation: The Aruba Island rattlesnake, *Crotalus unicolor*, is an endangered species which has proven to be easily bred in captivity

DIADEM SNAKE

The diadem snake, *Spalaerosophis diadema*, is a little-known species from North Africa, the Middle East, Pakistan and India. It grows to almost 2 m (6½ ft) in length and, although coloration varies somewhat according to the place of origin (and subspecies), it tends to be tan to brown in colour with a series of brown blotches down the back. The subspecies *S. d. atriceps* develops variable black markings with age, often on the head but also on parts of the body. *S. d. cliffordi* is the subspecies most often available and this form is found in North Africa and the Middle East.

The care is as for ratsnakes (genus *Elaphe*). The temperament of this species varies considerably: some specimens are tractable and easy to handle while others are aggressive and difficult to manage. Breeding follows the same general pattern as for ratsnakes and most other colubrids. A clutch of about 6-10 eggs is laid in the spring or summer. Second clutches can probably be expected, but this species has not been bred to any great extent.

DISEASES

Maintaining a collection of snakes in good health is largely a matter of choosing healthy animals to start with, and creating a satisfactory environment for them. Although they can suffer from a variety of diseases and parasites, snakes are, in general, very hardy animals which will live for many years without any need for veterinary treatment. Before acquiring new animals, the notes on QUARANTINE should be read carefully. If the animal has been taken from the wild, it is quite likely that it will be harbouring a number of internal and external parasites, but regular cleaning, together with the feeding of clean cage-bred rodents, will usually break the life-cycle of these, with the result that, after a month or two, the snake should be clear of all infections or infestations.

Signs that a snake is suffering from ill-health include all or some of the following:

Refusal to feed This is not necessarily due to infection, many snakes suffer stress when first caged and may refuse food for several weeks. Snakes often refuse food when they are about to shed their skin, males may refuse food in the spring when they are more interested in mating, and many snakes lose their appetite at the end of the summer when they are preparing for hibernation. If none of these applies, and the correct conditions, especially temperature and somewhere to hide, are provided, normal feeding will usually be resumed.

Regurgitation Again, this is not always a sign of disease since snakes will sometimes regurgitate their food after a day or two if the temperature is too high or too low, if they are handled roughly or otherwise disturbed, or if the meal has proved too large for them to digest. If the conditions are corrected, the snake will usually feed and digest its food normally, but at least one week should be allowed to elapse before further feeding is attempted and the next meal should be about half the usual size for that individual. Repeated regurgitation may indicate a problem and veterinary advice should be sought.

Abnormal faeces Liquid or slimy faeces, faeces which are green in colour or are accompanied by a bad odour may be a sign that the snake is suffering from an intestinal infection – seek veterinary advice. The presence of worms in the faeces is an obvious sign of infestation and if a low-powered microscope is available, the eggs of worms may be checked for.

Incomplete skin-shedding This is often caused by conditions which are too dry (see SKIN-SHEDDING and HUMIDITY), but is occasionally a sign that the general health of the snake is not good.

Erratic movement Certain diseases cause the snake's movements to become erratic or the snake itself to take up unnatural positions, e.g. the head held up as if the snake is looking at the sky. At other times the snake will go into convulsions. These problems may be associated with the central nervous system and are sometimes caused by serious parasite infestations, so veterinary advice should be sought. Snakes which lack muscle tone and which hang limply when picked up may be suffering from calcium deficiency, which can often be corrected by the addition of calcium and vitamins to their diet (see FEEDING) although a complete cure may take many months or even years to be totally effective.

Abnormal behaviour A snake-keeper who is 'in tune' with his or her animals will soon learn to recognise abnormal behaviour. These, often subtle, changes in behaviour are often early-warning signals that a problem has arisen, and the problem can often be corrected before the animal becomes clinically ill simply by checking and adjusting the snake's environment.

Although the diseases and parasites of reptiles are not well known compared with those of other groups of animals, certain of the more common ones occur repeatedly and are therefore worth mentioning. Snakes which are suffering from anything except the most minor problems should be taken to a vet, who will have facilities for examining the animal, isolating the bacterium or virus concerned and conducting sensitivity tests on it. In this way, the correct drug and dosage can be scientifically prescribed.

Respiratory infection Snakes which sneeze, or have large quantities of mucus in their mouths or blocked nostrils may be suffering from bacterial infection. The problem may correct itself if the snake is kept in a warm draught-free environment with clean drinking water available at all times. If it does not clear up, veterinary advice should be sought.

Salmonella infection A number of strains of *Salmonella* bacteria have been found in snakes and severe infections can cause digestive problems, usually signified by slimy, greenish faeces, accompanied by a bad smell. Treatment with an antibiotic, after veterinary consultation, is usually quite straightforward.

Gastro-enteritis This disease is caused by an amoeba, *Entamoeba invadens*, which lives in the digestive system. It can rapidly lead to the death of the snake. Symptoms are regurgitation, and faeces which are whitish and surrounded by large quantities of mucus. It is highly infectious and snakes suspected of suffering from gastro-enteritis should be isolated immediately. Drugs are available to treat this disease but rapid diagnosis and treatment are essential.

Worms A number of parasitic worms may be found in the intestinal and respiratory systems of snakes. Under normal circumstances these do not create a serious health problem, but if the snake is under stress their populations may grow to unacceptable levels. Treatment with worming tablets (dissolved in water and introduced through a syringe and rubber tube in the case of small snakes, or hidden in the food in the case of larger ones) is usually effective and the dosage rates recommended for dogs and cats can be applied to snakes.

Mites Snake mites live on the scales of the snake and lay their eggs in crevices, especially around the eyes. They are dark brown and quite large and can easily be seen with the naked eye, moving around on the surface. The first sign of infestation, however, is often the presence of a white or pale grey dust on the snake's head – this is the mites' droppings. Although the mites do little harm themselves, they can transmit diseases from one snake to another and, in severe infestations, can lead to skin-shedding problems. They are easily eliminated by placing a small piece of pest-strip in a small, perforated container and hanging this in the cage for three days. One week later the procedure should be repeated in order to kill any mites which have hatched in the meantime, and a third treatment, after another week, can be carried out to be absolutely sure. Obviously, there is no point in eliminating mites from one cage if other, neighbouring snakes are also infested, and a thorough attempt should be made to rid the whole collection of mites at the same time.

   Note: there is some concern over the safety of dichlorvos, the active constituent in pest-strips, and care should be taken to dispose of it safely.

Injuries may be found on newly caught snakes or on snakes which have been roughly handled. Some will rub their noses raw in an attempt to escape from their cage when first captured and if this problem recurs then serious thought should be given to changing the materials from which the cage is made. Treatment of superficial wounds and injuries consists of dusting the affected area with sulfanilamide powder. In the case of wounds which have become secondarily infected with a bacterium, antibiotic powder or ointment may be necessary.

Snakes which have been exposed to a continually damp substrate, either in the wild or in captivity, often develop small blisters on their ventral surface. In extreme cases, the edges of the ventral scales turn brown and begin to rot away due to a secondary infection. Treatment consists of correcting the conditions and, if necessary, applying sulfanilamide powder or a cream containing antibiotic or antiseptic substances.

DISINFECTANTS

The purpose of a disinfectant is to prevent the build-up of bacteria and viruses on inert surfaces (i.e. on cages and water bowls, etc.) and to reduce the chances of cross-infection between animals. Although there are several types of disinfectant, and very many brands, a stock of one or two will usually serve for the majority of purposes. It is important to realise that most disinfectants become neutralised in the presence of organic material. Therefore, all traces of faeces and bedding must be thoroughly washed before the disinfectant can be used effectively. Warm soapy water is the best method of achieving this and, although some of the more expensive disinfectants are combined with a detergent so that cleaning and disinfection can be carried out in a single operation, separate washing before disinfection is still recommended.

For general sterilisation of cages and waterbowls, a chlorine-based disinfectant, such as sodium hypochlorite, is perfectly adequate and should form the main general-purpose disinfectant in all collections. Several brands are cheaply available as household disinfectant or, in lower concentrations, as preparations for sterilising babies' feeding bottles. Cheap household bleach is suitable for most applications: it should be used as a 3-5 per cent solution and the cage or bowl left to soak for an hour or so, after which it should be rinsed thoroughly in cold water. Any remaining traces of chlorine will dissipate as the object dries. Note, however, that household bleach is highly corrosive and should not be used on metal objects. Note also that coal tar derivatives, which are also sold as household disinfectants, are *not* suitable for animal equipment as they can be toxic.

Many disinfectants are based on ampholytic surface agents. These compounds leave a thin layer of disinfectant over the object so that their benefit continues after they have been rinsed off. Although they are not as effective in killing viruses and spores as the chlorine-based compounds, they have wide applications and are not so corrosive. Note that it is possible to acquire an allergy to these chemicals, leading to dermatitis, and if this should occur a different type of disinfectant should be used.

Quaternary ammonium products are often recommended for water bowls, etc. as they are non-toxic. They are frequently combined with cleansing and deodorising substances which leave the objects smelling sweet.

Alcohols are strong disinfectants which are normally restricted to the sterilisation of instruments, etc. Thus sexing probes, feeding tongs, scrapers and so on should be left standing in a jar of one of these products when not in use, and 'dipped' after each cage is serviced in order to prevent cross-infection. This is usually superfluous in the average collection, but can be useful for servicing animals in quarantine (although a separate set of tools for each cage is even better). Alcohol-based disinfectants may also be used for cleaning the hands before and after handling diseased or newly acquired animals.

Iodine-based disinfectants can be identified by their yellowish-brown colour and are more commonly used as surgical scrubs in the veterinary profession. However, they can be effective in clearing up infections resulting from wounds and blisters on the surface of a snake, e.g. scale rot. This, of course, is outside the scope of their intended use as a disinfectant.

EGG-EATING SNAKE

The egg-eating snake, *Dasypeltis scabra*, is a medium-sized African colubrid, which is of interest mainly because of its feeding habits. It lives entirely on a diet of birds' eggs and has a series of specialised vertebrae with which it saws through the shells, regurgitating these as the contents of the egg are swallowed. Although the snake can attain a length of almost 1 m (3 ft), most specimens are considerably smaller than this. Their coloration is highly variable but most are some shade of grey or brown, with a row of darker blotches running along the back and with additional blotches on the flanks. Occasional specimens are unmarked.

Although harmless, an egg-eater might mimic the venomous night adder, *Causus rhombeatus*, when threatened. It will coil and uncoil its body rapidly, causing the rough scales to produce a rasping or hissing sound, and may make mock strikes, displaying the black interior of its mouth.

Care of this species could not be simpler, provided a constant supply of eggs is available! Although they have a remarkable gape and are capable of taking eggs which are far larger in diameter than their heads, young snakes must be fed on small eggs such as those of finches, not easily available unless you know of someone who breeds these birds. As they grow they will graduate to quails', pigeons' and even chickens' eggs. An alternative way of feeding them is to introduce egg yolk straight into their stomach using a syringe and rubber tube, but this rather counteracts one of the main reasons for keeping them.

A temperature of about 25°C (77°F) seems to suit them well, although they should be offered a range of temperatures. If breeding is intended, it will probably be necessary to lower the temperature during the winter, although, as yet, this species has not been bred regularly because of the obvious drawback of finding a suitable food supply for the small (20 cm/8 in) hatchlings.

EGG-LAYING

Snakes which lay eggs must be given a suitable substrate in which to deposit them. It must be clean and damp, and placed in a part of the cage in which the snake will feel secure, i.e. not directly under a light. One of the best arrangements is to take an appropriately sized plastic food container with a snap-on lid in which a small hole has been cut. The container is then three-quarters filled with moist peat, sand or moss and placed in the cage about one week before the female is due to lay, so that she can get used to going into it. Very large snakes, especially those which brood their eggs, may decline the use of a laying box and merely select a suitable part of the cage in which to lay their eggs.

Laying will take place one to two weeks after the snake sheds its skin (this is known as the pre-laying shed) and, usually, four to six weeks after mating (although this depends on several factors such as the species involved, temperature, etc). Snakes which are forming eggs will become swollen and cylindrical in cross-section. Often the skin becomes stretched and is visible between the scales in the rear half of the body. As egg-laying approaches the bulge will move down the body until the unlaid eggs are concentrated in the rear third, immediately in front of the tail. Some large snakes, especially pythons, will warm the eggs by adopting strange positions in the cage, sometimes lying completely upside down if this results in bringing the eggs closer to the heat source. This activity is natural and should not give cause for alarm (although it often does!).

Quite often, snakes which look as though they are forming eggs suddenly become thinner just before laying and this can cause confusion ('is she or isn't she going to lay?'), but if in doubt, a laying box should be placed in the cage anyway, otherwise the eggs will be laid on the bedding (and may dry out) or in the water bowl (and drown). As soon as the eggs are laid they should be taken out, set up in a clean box with vermiculite and placed in the incubator (see INCUBATING EGGS).

The only possible deviations from this process involve those species of pythons which brood their eggs throughout incubation, especially the Burmese and Indian pythons, *Python molurus*. Here, the eggs *can* be removed to the incubator as usual, but it will be more interesting to leave them with the female. She will coil around them and adjust her body to regulate their temperature and humidity. It will be necessary to spray water into the cage with a fine mister every day, or to make some other arrangement for the maintenance of the correct humidity. The females of some species twitch

spasmodically while brooding their eggs and this is thought to raise the temperature somewhat. The female may leave the pile of eggs to drink and to feed, although individuals vary. When the eggs are about to hatch (or if they are infertile) she will abandon them. If this occurs before the full incubation period has been completed, and the eggs look as though they are still developing, they should be removed to an incubator immediately. (Some females fail to incubate their eggs successfully, usually due to stress of some sort.) Newly imported females, i.e. those which are carrying eggs when they arrive at their destination, rarely make 'good mothers', and it is probably safer under these circumstances to take the eggs away as soon as they are laid.

EGGS

Most snakes lay eggs. These are unlike the eggs of birds in that their shells are pliable and allow the passage of air and water, which are essential to the developing embryo. In addition, snake eggs do not need to be turned (although accidental turning should not affect the hatch-rate).

The number of eggs laid in a clutch will depend on the snake concerned. In general, large species lay more eggs than small species, and, within species, large females lay more eggs than small females. In some cases, as females grow, they lay more eggs, in others, they lay

A female Sinaloan milksnake, *Lampropeltis triangulum sinaloae*, laying her eggs

larger eggs. Usually there is a trade-off and both the clutches and their eggs become slightly larger. Naturally, females in good condition will lay better clutches than those which are sick, under stress or thin. Furthermore, females of many species are capable of laying more than one clutch during a breeding season if they are well cared for. In order for second clutches to be laid successfully, the female should be helped to regain her normal body weight as soon as possible after laying the first clutch. Usually, this involves giving her four or five good feeds after laying, then placing her with the male while continuing to feed her regularly. Unfortunately, some females refuse to feed as soon as the eggs start to develop, although most will continue to feed right up to egg-laying. (See also EGG-LAYING and INCUBATING EGGS.) (**In colour on page 54.**)

F

FEEDING

People who are used to dealing with normal household pets sometimes experience difficulty in coming to terms with animals which often go several weeks without food! Snakes are opportunistic feeders which have evolved to fast for long periods. In addition, they do not use metabolic processes to maintain a high body temperature (see THERMOREGULATION) and thus make much more efficient use of their food than mammals and birds.

This does not mean that snakes can be neglected, however, and a suitable feeding regime is one of the most important factors in keeping and breeding them successfully. Practically all of the snakes which are likely to be kept as captives will be rodent-eaters. (Except where stated otherwise, all species described and recommended in this book eat mice or rats.) Therefore a regular and reliable supply of mice of the appropriate size must be arranged before any snake is purchased. A large collection of snakes, especially one in which quantities of hatchlings are produced each year, may warrant the setting up of a rodent breeding colony. Techniques for such an operation should be researched elsewhere, but it is appropriate here to mention that breeding mice and rats is an onerous and labour-intensive task, and that the animals concerned must be maintained under hygienic and humane conditions, regardless of the fact that they are intended as food. The same obviously goes for batches of live mice, etc. purchased in bulk for feeding purposes. Laboratory-type cages, with water bottles and feeding hoppers, are far preferable to makeshift cages adapted from discarded aquaria, etc. Food animals should be humanely killed before they are fed to the snakes.

The simplest and most cost-effective way of feeding snakes is to accustom them to eating dead prey which has been stored in a deep-freeze. Each item must be thoroughly thawed and may at first be jiggled in front of the snake on the end of long feeding forceps in order to encourage the snake to eat. Very quickly, the snake will accept dead prey placed in the cage without any manipulation. For difficult snakes, see under the heading FEEDING HATCHLINGS. The techniques used to encourage hatchling snakes to feed can also be employed with adults, although they will rarely be needed if healthy, preferably captive-bred stock has been obtained.

Mice and rats, if bred or kept alive until needed, must be given suitable accommodation and provided with food and water at all times. Laboratory cages are the best choice

Refusal to feed can be due to a variety of causes. The snake may be about to shed its skin (some will continue to feed at this time, but others will not). If it is a female, it may be about to lay (again, many will continue to feed). It may be too cold, or some other aspect of its environment may be unsuitable (check the conditions). It may feel insecure (provide a hide-box and place the food inside it). It may be under stress (usually due to one of the above). It may not be hungry (most snakes eat once or twice a week but some will refuse food for a while if they have been overfed). It may have ceased feeding in expectation of a period of hibernation (see HIBERNATION). It may be sick. Continued refusal to feed, assuming that suitable food has been offered and the conditions are correct, means a trip to the vet in order to check the health of the snake and possibly to give it a vitamin injection in order to stimulate its appetite – this should rarely be necessary.

Some species will not eat rodents and obviously other arrangements will have to be made to cater for these. Insectivorous snakes are fairly easily dealt with as many reptile and tropical bird dealers supply mealworms, crickets and so on, and additional variety can be provided by collecting spiders, etc. (although you must make sure that such invertebrates have not been contaminated by insecticides). Species which eat frogs, toads or lizards are not (or should not be) offered for sale. Some species can be gradually 'weaned' away from their natural diet and onto mice if the mouse is first flavoured with the natural prey. This is achieved by placing the dead mouse in a cage with a live lizard, frog, etc. or using a dead animal to transfer its scent to the mouse by rubbing it over the mouse's snout. However, by far the best advice is to stick to species which eat food which is easily obtained.

Garter snakes, water snakes and their relatives prefer to eat amphibians but can often be persuaded to eat fish or, in some cases, earthworms. If fish is fed to these snakes it must be of a type which does not contain the enzyme thiaminase, which will destroy the thiamine (Vitamin B1) in the snake's body, leading to loss of muscle control and, eventually, death. Goldfish and trout are two species which seem to constitute a suitable diet, with none of the above drawbacks.

Alternatively, any species of fish can be used provided that extra Vitamin B1 is sprinkled on the food to counteract the effect of the enzyme, or the fish is heated to 80°C (175°F) for five minutes, which deactivates the enzyme. Snakes of this type are normally very accommodating when it comes to feeding, and there is no reason why a purely artificial diet could not be used,

which could include all the necessary vitamins and minerals as well as flavourings to make the substance palatable. As interest in snakes of this group grows, formulae for such diets should become commercially available.

FEEDING HATCHLINGS

Snakes of several species which are offered for sale are sometimes reluctant to take mice straightaway. This applies especially to hatchlings because the young of many species would normally feed on young lizards in the wild, and graduate to rodents as they grew. (They hatch at the same time as lizards do and these form an abundant food source.)

Most of the species which are occasionally 'picky' belong to the genus *Lampropeltis* (kingsnakes and milksnakes), and include Mexican kings (*L. mexicana*), grey-banded kings (*L. alterna*), mountain kings (*L. pyromelana, L. ruthveni* and *L. zonata*), and some of the smaller subspecies of milksnakes (*L. triangulum*). Very often, hatchlings of these species are well supplied with food reserves at the time of hatching and are simply not hungry, so refusal to feed at first should not necessarily be cause for alarm. If the snake has not fed voluntarily after one month, or if it begins to look thin before this, then some tricks may have to be used to encourage it to start feeding. Usually, the hard part is getting the snake to take its first mouse meal. Once it has done this there should be no further trouble.

First make sure that the conditions are right for the snake, especially with respect to temperature (see HATCHLINGS and TEMPERATURE), before going through the following sequence of techniques:

1   Many snakes like to feed in an enclosed space, so put a small cardboard or plastic box in the cage, with a hole just big enough for the snake to get through. Then put a dead newborn mouse in the box.

2   If this does not work, do the same thing with a live newborn mouse.

3   Next, try a dead newborn mouse which has had its nose damaged after death – it is surprising how often this is effective.

4   If none of these techniques work, the next trick is to try to fool the snake into thinking that the mouse is a lizard. Wash it in water to remove as much mouse smell as possible and then rub it over a lizard. If you do not have a live one handy, obtain a dead lizard from a reptile supplier, freeze it and use it several times. Go through all the procedures listed above in turn.

5   If the snake still has not fed, and nine times out of ten it will have, it is time to try some

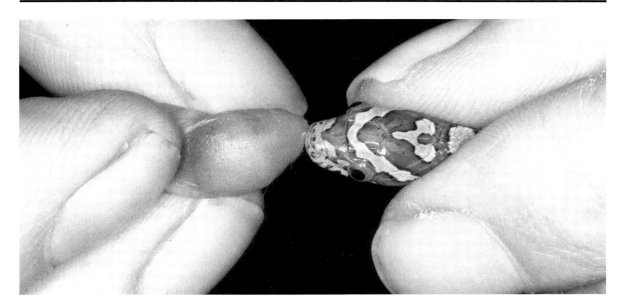

gentle persuasion. Grasp the snake just behind the head and use the mouse's snout to force its mouth open. Push the mouse well into the snake's mouth then let the snake bite on it. Keep hold of the snake and tug the mouse slightly to hook the snake's teeth into it. Now gently replace the snake into its cage and hold your breath. You may have to repeat this procedure several times before the snake eventually begins to swallow the mouse. As soon as it does, put a second mouse in the cage. The snake's appetite will be stimulated by now and it will probably be ready to take another mouse voluntarily.

6   The last resort is to force-feed the snake. Start as before, but when the mouse is in the

Snakes which refuse to take food voluntarily must be force-fed. Here a dead mouse is being used to open the mouth of a small corn snake

Having grasped the mouse, the snake will usually continue to swallow on its own if it is gently put back into its cage

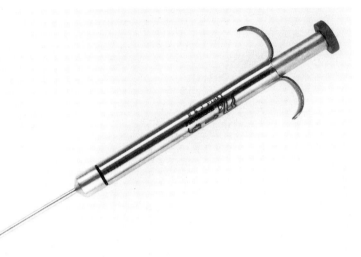

'Pinky-pumps', or pinky processors, should be used only as a last resort. Macerated mouse is forced through the nozzle which is inserted well down the snake's throat. Great care must be taken not to damage the snake or cause unnecessary stress

snake's mouth push it gently into its throat with a very blunt instrument. Keeping pushing until the mouse has disappeared from sight, then massage the snake's throat until the mouse has been worked back into the stomach (about one-third of the way along the snake).

An alternative way of force-feeding is to use a 'pinky pump', which is a syringe-like instrument, designed to homogenise the mouse as it is forced through the nozzle, and thus 'inject' semi-fluid mouse into the snake's throat. Pinky pumps are essential for feeding species which are too small at hatching to eat even the youngest mice. These species include several of the North American milksnakes, such as *L. t. amaura* and *L. t. gentilis*. Otherwise, they should be used only as a last resort, i.e. in order to keep a snake alive until it begins to feed voluntarily.

Just in case the above list of gruesome instructions has put the reader off the idea of raising baby snakes, it is worth pointing out that these measures are only necessary in a small minority of cases. Common kingsnakes and prairie king snakes (*Lampropeltis getulus* and *L. calligaster*) hardly ever refuse to eat pink mice, nor do the larger forms of milksnake or any of the ratsnakes or gopher snakes, and these are the species recommended to beginners. On the other hand, some of the 'picky' species are very attractive, and most experienced snake-keepers would consider them well worth the extra trouble.

FLYING SNAKES

Several species of rear-fanged colubrids are popularly known as flying snakes, and of these *Chrysopelea ornata* and *C. paradisi* are occasionally kept in captivity. The latter is also sometimes known as the paradise tree snake. Both are elongated, slender tree snakes which are capable of launching themselves from high branches and gliding to a lower perch if alarmed. They do this by lifting their rib-cage and making the ventral surface of their body slightly concave. Both are green in colour, with black-edged scales giving a netted appearance. Some individuals of *C. ornata* have scattered red scales.

Although beautiful, these snakes generally make poor captives. They often arrive in bad condition and can be difficult to induce to feed. Although some will take rodents, others will only accept lizards and this, coupled with their often aggressive temperaments, makes them unsuitable for private collections. Although they produce a venom, their fangs are situated well back in the mouth and they are harmless to humans. They have been bred in captivity, but the young require force-feeding (or a diet of small lizards) for a considerable period before they will accept newborn mice voluntarily. They are therefore best left to the specialist.

G

GARTER SNAKES

Of the numerous species and subspecies of garter snakes (genus *Thamnophis*), found throughout North and Central America, relatively few forms are easily available, and there is little interest in maintaining them other than as an expendable pet shop item. This is an unfortunate situation since they form an interesting and attractive group, and can make a welcome change from typical rodent-eating, secretive colubrids and boids. They are active foragers, often in semi-aquatic habitats, and feed largely upon fish and amphibians. Some species specialise in earthworms, while a few will eat rodents when adult.

They require relatively larger cages than most colubrids of the same size, and the plastic box system does not lend itself particularly well to their maintenance; they seem to do better in large glass cages, or wooden boxes with glass fronts. Newborn young, however, can be kept in smaller plastic boxes. The usual arrangement of heating, giving a thermal gradient, is necessary, and these are among the few species of snake which will bask in the heat given off by a light bulb or spotlight, although this is not strictly essential. The temperature range should be 20-30°C (68-86°F) in the summer, with a distinct drop in temperature in the winter if you hope to breed them. This is probably not essential for all forms, but helps to synchronise the mating behaviour of the males and the females. They appreciate a large water bowl in which they can submerge themselves completely, but the substrate must be kept dry at all times otherwise they quickly develop sores and blisters on their undersides.

Food requirements are rather more difficult to arrange than with rodent-eating species. They are most easily raised on fish, using species such as guppies for the hatchlings and graduating up to goldfish for adults. Most will accept thawed fish in the form of whitebait, lance fish and so on, but the note under FEEDING, regarding vitamin deficiencies when this type of food is used, should be read carefully. A few of the more robust species will take young mice once they are large enough to do so, and this is, generally speaking, a much more satisfactory diet for them.

Garter snakes give birth to live young, after mating in the spring and carrying the developing embryos for several months until they are ready to be born in late summer or autumn. The clutch size varies considerably with species, and sometimes with subspecies, but has been recorded as up to 100 for exceptionally large females. However, 10–20 is a more usual number. The young should be segregated from the adults, but may be kept in small groups for rearing. Care should be taken when feeding them on worms as two individuals frequently start to swallow opposite ends of the same worm and then one will engulf the other when they meet in the middle. They can either be fed individually, or feeding sessions can be supervised, with a pair of fine scissors at the ready. They grow rapidly with adequate feeding and can be ready to breed by the following spring, i.e. after eight to ten months' growth. Care of all species is similar, and only the most commonly encountered will be listed.

Western ribbon snake, *Thamnophis sauritus*. Ribbon snakes do not generally make such good pets as garter snakes

Thamnophis marcianus – **Chequered Garter Snake (In colour on page 27.)**
This is a robust and attractive species in which the background is cream or tan, the central stripe pale cream or white and the area between chequered with large black blotches. There is invariably a black collar, often broken by the dorsal stripe. This is a common species which does very well in captivity. Adults can usually be persuaded to take mice, and may grow very stocky. Small litters of about 12 young are born and these are equally robust, taking earthworms and/or small fish or chopped fish.

Thamnophis sirtalis – **Common Garter Snake**
This species has the largest range of the North American species and is found in some form or another from coast to coast. It is divided into a number of distinct subspecies, which vary greatly in their coloration and their abundance. All grow to a maximum of 1 m (3 ft), but are usually smaller than this. They are characterised by three longitudinal stripes, one down the centre of the back and one on each flank. These may be almost any colour, depending on location, and sometimes the central stripe is different in colour from those on the flanks. The ease with which this species adapts to captivity seems to depend on its origin. The west coast forms are often more robust than those from the east, and more inclined to switch to a diet of mice once they grow large enough. However, these subspecies have smaller litters, on average, usually about 12 as opposed to 30 or more for the eastern varieties. The most notable subspecies are:

Thamnophis sirtalis concinnus Red-spotted garter snake
This form occurs along the north-eastern coast of North America. This is a very attractive subspecies with a red head, pale blue stripes on a black background and red bars on either side of the dorsal stripe. It usually does very well in captivity.

Thamnophis sirtalis parietalis Red-sided garter snake
This subspecies is similar to the red-spotted subspecies but not so brightly coloured, lacking the red head and the bluish tinge to the stripes. Its range extends up into Canada and it is very tolerant of cold conditions. Huge numbers of this subspecies are collected each spring as they emerge from their communal hibernation dens. These find their way into the pet trade where they retail at low prices. In this way they are often the spark which starts a sustained interest in snake-keeping, although many obviously perish at the hands of beginners, since they are not among the easiest snakes to keep in the long term.

Thamnophis sirtalis similis Florida garter snake
This is a large subspecies with an overall bluish wash to its otherwise grey coloration. (**In colour on page 27.**)

Thamnophis sirtalis sirtalis Eastern garter snake
This is a highly variable form, and may be grey, brown or reddish with paler stripes. Populations of jet-black snakes of this subspecies are found in one or two localities in the north of the range. These are especially attractive and are one of the few garter snake types to be bred in captivity. They tend to be tougher than other forms. (**In colour on page 27.**)

Thamnophis sirtalis tetrataenia San Francisco garter snake
The San Francisco garter snake is fully protected by law and is only mentioned here because it demonstrates the ease with which numbers of rare species can be dramatically increased by captive-breeding. Breeding nuclei have been established in several North American zoos and these all breed regularly, providing a small but steady supply of fresh stock. The subspecies is spectacularly marked with cream stripes, bordered by black and separated by a wide red area. The head is also red.

Thamnophis radix – **Plains Garter Snake**
This species is not often seen, although it is one of the prettiest and easiest to care for. It is black with an orange dorsal stripe and pale green stripes on the flanks. It can produce up to 50 young, which will accept earthworms as well as fish.
Note: ribbon snakes, *Thamnophis sauritus* and *T. proximus*, although belonging to the same genus as the garter snakes, are somewhat different. They are much more slender in shape and most will not accept earthworms. Moreover, some will not take fish either, and insist on a diet of amphibians, making their upkeep rather tricky. They have small litters of up to six very slender young which are difficult to rear.

GLOSSY SNAKES (In colour on page 30.)

The glossy snake, *Arizona elegans*, has a wide distribution in North America, where a number of subspecies are recognised, although many of these are difficult to distinguish unless good locality data are available. All grow to about 1 m (3 ft), sometimes slightly more, and are cream or pale grey in colour with tan or brown blotches. The overall pale coloration gives a faded or 'washed out' look. They are closely related to the gopher snakes (genus *Pituophis*) and the ratsnakes (genus *Elaphe*) from which they differ in having smooth shiny scales. This species seems never to bite, even when first captured, unlike many of the gopher snakes.

Glossy snakes usually do very well in captivity, readily accepting mice in lieu of their natural diet which probably consists largely of lizards. They are nocturnal desert snakes which may be treated in exactly the same way as the gopher snakes, ratsnakes, etc., although breeding data are scarce since, for some reason, they have not attracted much attention from snake-keepers. It is safe to assume that the conditions required to induce breeding in related species also apply to this one.

GOPHER SNAKES

Under this heading are included all snakes of the genus *Pituophis*, even although many of them are also known by common names other than gopher snake. At present, only two species are recognised, one of which, *P. deppi*, is from Mexico and the other, *P. melanoleucus*, has a huge distribution throughout most of North America. In eastern North America the various subspecies are commonly known as pine snakes, in the central states the predominant form is known as the bull snake and in the west several subspecies are known collectively as gopher snakes. It seems likely that some of these forms are distinct enough to warrant full species status, and taxonomic changes may take place in the future.

The wide variety of forms in this genus provides plenty of scope for an interesting collection, and several of the subspecies have produced albino or amelanistic strains. Maximum size varies with subspecies, but may be as much as 2 m (6½ ft) in some cases. Large gopher snakes are impressive snakes and wild-caught adults can often be somewhat interesting to try to handle! However, most are available as captive-bred hatchlings and these adapt well to captivity. They should be kept on a thermal gradient with an opportunity to reach 25-30°C (77-86°F) at times. If it is intended to breed them, it will be necessary to reduce this during the winter months. All forms take rodents readily, and many produce large hatchlings which are capable of handling furred mice straightaway. Because of the great variation between subspecies, more detailed information is given in the following accounts.

Pituophis melanoleucus
GROUP 1

WESTERN FORMS

(GOPHER SNAKES AND THE BULL SNAKE)

Pituophis melanoleucus affinis – Sonoran Gopher Snake (**In colour on page 30.**)
One of the smaller forms, with dark brown to rust-coloured blotches along the back and flanks on a cream or yellow background. Although wild individuals may hiss and strike, this is, in general, one of the easier forms to handle. It lays clutches of eight to ten eggs and the hatchlings are about 40 cm (16 in) in size. They will take mice up to one week old immediately. An albino strain is available which is lemon yellow and white in colour.

Pituophis melanoleucus annectans – San Diego Gopher Snake
Similar in size to the Sonoran gopher snake, the San Diego gopher is rather darker in overall colour and its blotches are smaller and closer together, often joining at their edges. Albino strains are white and orange, and the care of either type is exactly as for the Sonoran subspecies.

Pituophis melanoleucus catenifer – Pacific Gopher Snake
This is an even darker version of the previous form. In some areas a naturally occurring striped phase crops up occasionally, in which the dark markings are arranged as longitudinal streaks instead of blotches. Albino strains of both the blotched and striped form are available

Pituophis melanoleucus deserticola – Great Basin Gopher Snake
This is similar to the Sonoran gopher snake, but with darker and more extensive blotching. Again, an albino strain is available.

Pituophis melanoleucus pumilus – Santa Cruz Gopher Snake
This is a dwarf island race, similar in appearance to the San Diego gopher snake, but growing to only 1 m (3 ft) in length. Its care and breeding are similar to the other gopher snakes.

Pituophis melanoleucus sayi – Bull Snake
This is the largest subspecies, and may be the

Hognose Snakes

Plains hognose snake,
*Heterodon nasicus
nasicus*

Dusty hognose snake,
Heterodon nasicus gloydi

Miscellaneous
Colubrid Snakes

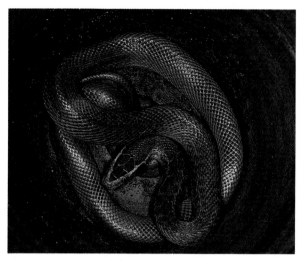

Brown house snake, *Lamprophis fuliginosus*, a tough and easy-to-keep species from Africa

Lyre snake, *Trimorphodon biscutatus*

Florida indigo snake *Drymarchon corais couperi*

The plain-coloured form of the Florida pine snake,
Pituophis melanoleucus mugitus

largest snake in North America, regularly
growing to over 2 m (6½ ft). It is variable in
colour, being yellow, cream or tan with blotches
of brown or reddish-brown. The bull snake has
a reputation for being bad-tempered, but is
probably no worse in this respect than the other
subspecies: captive-bred young tame easily and
do very well in captivity. Care and breeding are
as above, but large females may produce
clutches of up to 15 eggs. An albino strain is
available

Pituophis melanoleucus vertebralis – Cape
Gopher Snake
This is a Mexican subspecies found only in the
Cape Region of Baja California. In general
appearance this is a typical gopher snake, but
it differs from the other forms in having a large
amount of orange or red between the blotches,
especially towards the tail. An intermediate
subspecies, *P. m. bimaris*, is found further
north in Baja California, but this seems to have
been largely overlooked by snake-breeders.

EASTERN SUBSPECIES

(PINE SNAKES)

Pituophis melanoleucus lodingi – Black Pine
Snake
As its name suggests, this subspecies is totally
black, although some specimens are dark brown
rather than jet-black. This form is rare in the
wild and not as prolific in captivity as the
western forms, usually laying small clutches of
four to six very large eggs. The hatchlings may
measure up to 45 cm (18 in) in total length and
feed readily on young mice.

Pituophis melanoleucus melanoleucus –
Northern Pine Snake (**In colour on page 30.**)
Another large and impressive pine snake, this
subspecies is white with irregular blotches of
dark brown or black. Some individuals have an
overall reddish tinge. Care and breeding is as
for the other subspecies, but this form also has
small clutches of very large eggs.

Pituophis melanoleucus mugitus – Florida Pine Snake

This subspecies is like a paler, more indistinctly marked version of *P. m. melanoleucus*. An interesting natural variation occurs in which the markings are absent and the snake is plain beige in colour. Heterozygous animals have marked heads and foreparts of the body, with the markings gradually fading away towards the tail – the variation is not, therefore, controlled by simple Mendelian inheritance (see SELECTIVE BREEDING). Care of this species is similar to that of other pine and gopher snakes.

Pituophis deppi – Mexican Gopher Snake

This gopher snake is classified as separate from the more northern forms, although its general appearance is similar. The subspecies usually offered for sale is *P. d. jani*. There is little information on its care or breeding although there is no reason to believe that its requirements are in any way different from the more familiar forms.

GREEN SNAKES (In colour on page 31.)

Two species of green snakes (genus *Opheodryas*) are found in North America, with at least two others hailing from Asia. However, the only species which is both freely available and easily kept is the rough green snake, *Opheodryas aestivus*. This is a pretty little snake, growing to a maximum of about 75 cm (30 in), but usually staying smaller than this. It is slender in build and plain green above, paler on the underside. The coloration of some individuals is brighter than others, but all are attractive when in good health.

This species can be kept in much the same way as other colubrids, i.e. in an individual box or cage with a heat gradient, but is also suitable for a display cage. It differs from most of the commonly kept species by eating insects, and will thrive if given a mixed diet consisting of crickets and waxworms, with the occasional addition of a spider. It should be fed more often than most other snakes, and it is a good idea to ensure that some food is present in the cage at all times, much in the way a lizard would be kept.

Several individuals may be kept together in a large glass cage, and this should be fairly tall since they like to climb. If a branch or piece of root is arranged beneath a heat source (for instance, a spotlight) they will spend most of their time basking. However, underfloor heating, in the form of a heat pad, should also be installed in order to provide a background temperature at night, etc. If a suitable light source can be found, it is even possible to grow living plants (in pots) in a vivarium with this species, provided that they are stout enough to withstand the weight of the snakes, and grow fast enough to counteract the depredations of crickets.

The reproductive cycle of this species is similar to that of other North American colubrids which mate in the spring and lay eggs in the summer. Clutches consist of a small number (about five) of elongated eggs. These hatch after an incubation period which appears to be subject to some variation, but which is invariably short. Care should be taken to remove the eggs before they are found by uneaten crickets, otherwise they will be destroyed. Better still, gravid females should be removed to a separate cage for egg-laying or alternative food should be used during the breeding season.

Notes: *Opheodryas vernalis*, the other North American species, is known as the smooth green snake. It is rather smaller than its rough relative, and tends to do less well in captivity. *Opheodryas major*, which comes from South East Asia, is much larger and has a yellow underside. Few of these are imported and there is little information on their long-term suitability as captives. Almost all *Opheodryas* offered for sale will be *O. aestivus*.

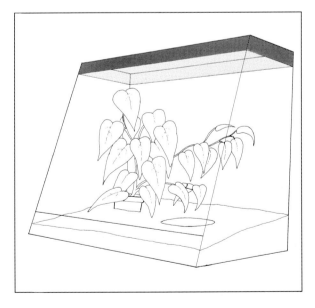

A tall cage with a robust potted plant makes an attractive and suitable cage for small semi-arboreal species such as rough green snakes

Breeding

Female dusty hognose snake with her eggs

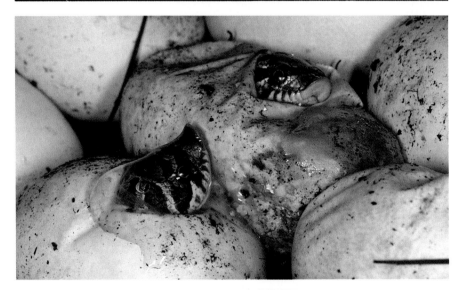

Hatchling hognose snakes emerging from their eggs

A batch of newly hatched Honduran milksnakes

Kingsnakes (1): Grey-banded and Prairie Kingsnakes

Grey-banded kingsnake,
Lampropeltis alterna
(Blair's phase)

Grey-banded kingsnake,
Lampropeltis alterna
(alterna phase)

Prairie kingsnake,
*Lampropeltis calligaster
calligaster*

H

HANDLING

Captive snakes should be handled as little as possible. Reasons for handling include removal from the cage for the purposes of cleaning, treatment with drugs, sexing or the removal of pieces of unshed skin. If snakes are obtained as hatchlings, they will quickly get used to occasional sympathetic handling and this will make life easier as they grow larger, but there is no reason to suppose that they ever 'like' to

be handled and it is a mistake to take them out of their cage for no other reason than to play with them.

Techniques for handling vary slightly according to the size and temperament of the snake. Juveniles of medium-sized species and small species are simply picked up around the mid-body and held firmly. For force-feeding or other manipulations, they should be held gently behind the head between the index finger and thumb. Larger snakes should have their body well supported along its length, otherwise injuries may result. For force-feeding, these snakes may require two people, or else the body can be tucked under an arm while the neck is held, leaving one hand free. Similarly, sexing with probes may require two people – one to

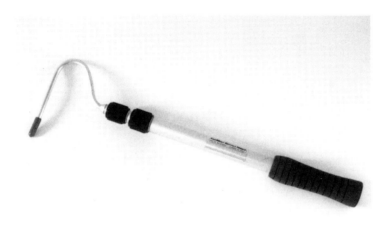

Snake hooks of various sizes are available and are useful for moving aggressive snakes. This model has a telescopic handle so that its length can be varied, and the hook can be packed away in a suitcase or rucksack

Holding a tame snake. The animal is well supported and there is no need to use unnecessary force to restrain it

hold the head and body while the other manipulates the probe.

Large, aggressive snakes, even non-venomous species, are best held firmly behind the neck at all times, with the rest of the body supported. They can first be pinned down *gently*, by placing a flexible dowel, or a purpose-made snake-hook across their neck (the traditional forked stick is totally useless). Many heavy-bodied species can simply be lifted off the ground by sliding a hook under their mid-body. Once they are off the ground they are much less likely to bite and can usually be held safely.

Venomous snakes are not dealt with to any great extent in this book for obvious reasons, but it should go without saying that these should always be moved about by using a long snake-hook or grab-stick. Furthermore, large boas and pythons are powerful snakes which can also be dangerous if not treated with respect. Never place a large specimen around the neck (either yours or anyone else's) and do not keep their cages at face level. Never go into large walk-in cages while the snake is feeding and make sure that the smell of rodents or other food items has been thoroughly washed off your hands before attempting to pick up a large constricting snake. Bites from large pythons and boas can be painful and serious, and there have been several cases where snakes have constricted their keeper during feeding sessions – sometimes with fatal results.

HATCHLINGS

The majority of captive-bred snakes purchased will be hatchlings. In addition, many snake-keepers are eventually successful in breeding from their adult snakes and are then faced with the task of accommodating the hatchlings. Many of the instructions given below for rearing hatchlings also apply to keeping snakes in general, but they are repeated here because young snakes are especially vulnerable to a bad environment. In other ways, however, hatchlings require rather different treatment from that described for adults.

Young snakes prefer small containers. These can be small plastic or glass aquaria, or plastic food containers (or shoe-boxes as they are known in the USA). As they grow they should gradually be moved on to slightly larger cages (rather like repotting a plant). It is best to keep the young snakes separate from each other while they are being reared, in order to avoid the possibility that they will damage, or even eat, one another during feeding. Their container should hold a suitable substrate, which may be soft wood shavings or two or three layers of paper. Small clay beads, such as

those used in horticulture, are more attractive, but they should be rinsed and dried before use to get rid of any dust, and changed as soon as they become soiled. Soil, peat, sand, etc. are not normally suitable substrates for snakes. In addition, a small water bowl and something for the snakes to hide in or under should be provided.

It is important that the bottom of the container is kept dry *at all times*. Failure to do this will result in sores and blisters on the underside of the snake and possibly respiratory diseases. In order to make sure that dampness does not occur, the cage should be well ventilated and the water bowl should only be about one-third full (this will avoid spillage if the snake decides to soak itself).

Heating should be provided *at one end of the cage only*. In this way a gradient will be created, allowing the snake to choose its own temperature. The most effective way of achieving this with small cages is to use a small, low-wattage heat tape, heating cable, heat pad or heat strip and to arrange the cage so that about one-third of it is over the pad. Several plastic containers can usually be heated by a single tape or strip, etc., and this provides a cheap and easy way of heating a small collection of young snakes (see HEATING for more details).

Most of the young snakes likely to be available will eat rodents. Baby snakes require a constant supply of baby mice and, as they grow, they will gradually move on to larger mice. Snakes vary in the amount of food they require but, on average, two mice each week is a good starting point. Snakes often refuse to feed if they are about to shed their skin, a state which can be recognised by an opaque, blue cast to the scales, especially noticeable over the eyes. Babies of some species are lizard-eaters in the wild and it may be difficult to persuade them to accept mice at first. There are ways around this problem, some of which are suggested under FEEDING HATCHLINGS, but beginners are advised to stick to those species which take baby mice readily.

In general, captive-bred snakes rarely suffer from diseases. When they do, the cause can usually be traced to an unsuitable environment, e.g. too cold, too damp, etc. Refusal to feed is usually the first sign of trouble. If a snake refuses food twice in a row, check the temperature, make sure that the snake has fresh water and a clean substrate and that it is not about to shed its skin. If these factors are not the cause of the problem (and usually they will be), consult a vet.

Kingsnakes (2): Forms of the Common Kingsnake

Californian kingsnake, *Lampropeltis getulus californiae*. This example is from the Mojave Desert. Snakes from this polulation are jet black and pure white and have more bands, on average, than snakes from other parts of the range

Californian kingsnake, *Lampropeltis getulus californiae*. This specimen, from near Tucson, has narrow white bands and is of the form sometimes known as '*yumensis*'

Blotched kingsnake, *Lampropeltis getulus goini*, a subspecies with a very restricted range in northern Florida

Speckled kingsnake,
*Lampropeltis getulus
holbrooki*

Mexican black kingsnake,
*Lampropeltis getulus
nigritus*

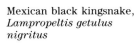

Desert kingsnake,
*Lampropeltis getulus
splendida*

HEATING

The thermal requirements of snakes and the way in which they regulate their temperature in the wild are described under the heading THERMOREGULATION. This section deals with the means by which these requirements can best be met, using a variety of equipment. If the notes on thermoregulation are read carefully it will be obvious that snakes kept at a constant temperature are not able to behave naturally. If heat is applied to the whole cage and the 'chosen' temperature (chosen by the *keeper*, not the snake) is unsuitable, the snake will be placed under stress, with serious results. Snakes can be kept in this way and many people do so successfully, but this does not mean it is the best way. If the snake is given a choice of temperatures within the cage, it can arrange to be in the right place at the right time *all the time*. This will vary according to whether it has just eaten, is about to shed its skin, whether it is night or day, etc. It is fairly safe to assume that snakes know better than humans how warm they need to be, so they should be given a choice.

As to the means of providing a choice, underfloor heating is ideally suited to this principle. The heat can be provided by a tape or cable positioned under *one end* of the cage or box and left on permanently (except when the animals are cooled off in the winter). This creates what is known as a thermal gradient and the snake will then sit over the cable if it needs to get warm, placing its body in contact with the warmest part of the cage. There is no need to incorporate a thermostat, except where there is a danger of overheating the entire cage. In this case the thermostat can be placed

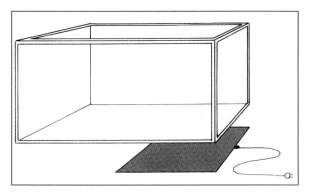

A small heat pad is the best method of heating a single cage. The pad is placed under one end only of the cage, allowing the snake to choose its preferred temperature by moving around within the cage

anywhere in the snake room, and set to trip at, say, 23°C (73°F). There is no need to heat the air in the vivarium, except in the case of the few highly arboreal species which are occasionally kept. This is also natural: the vast majority of snakes which are likely to end up in vivaria do not bask in the wild – ever. They are mostly active during the evening or early morning or are strictly nocturnal. They warm themselves by conduction (from the rock, sand or whatever it is that they are crawling over or sitting on), not by radiant heat. This rule applies to kingsnakes, ratsnakes, boas, pythons and most of the commonly kept snakes, with the possible exception of some of the garter snakes from northern climates, which may bask during the spring and autumn.

Installation of the appropriate equipment will depend on the numbers of snakes to be kept. One or two animals in cages are most efficiently heated by using a heat pad, or mat. These are wafer-thin and can be placed directly on a shelf with the cage resting on them. It is important to ensure that the type used is intended for use with vivaria, *not aquaria*, as the latter are too powerful. In order to produce the gradient required, the pad used should be about half the size of the cage and placed under one end only (or a pad can be used for two or more cages by placing the ends of several cages over part of the mat). If a large number of cages are to be heated, as in the rack system described under CAGES, then heating tape or cable can be used, and this is much more economical. Flat-sectioned tape is readily available in the USA, and is the favoured method. In the UK, cylindrical cable, designed for use as soil-warming cable, can be used. In either case, the tape or cable is laid along the shelf, if necessary in a rebate which is cut towards the back. The tape or cable should be flush with, or slightly below, the top of the shelf, so that the boxes can slide back over it.

If small lunch- or shoe-boxes are used, e.g. for

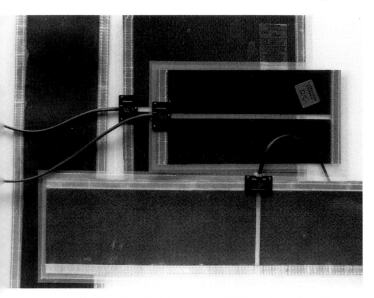

Heat pads and strips are available in a number of shapes and sizes to suit most applications

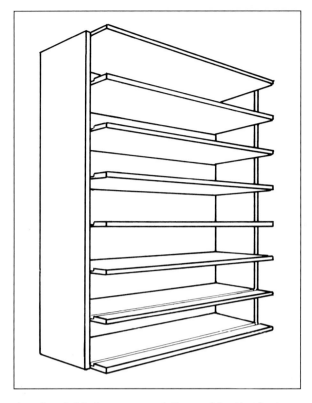

A rack suitable for accommodating and heating large numbers of small boxes, such as those containing a crop of hatchlings. This view is from the rear, showing the groove for a heat tape or cable running along the back of each shelf: by extending the shelves at the back, the cable can be removed and replaced quite easily

a 'crop' of hatchlings, a single cable or tape is sufficient, but where large snakes are housed in larger boxes it may be necessary to run two parallel cables in order to increase the warm area within the box. If these are controlled separately, either with a time-switch or manually, irregularities in the ambient temperature can also be catered to. Where the glass fronted cabinets are used, either with or

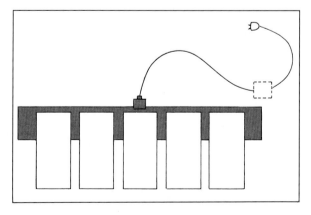

A heat strip can be used to heat several small boxes or cages containing snakes. Again, only one end of each box is in contact with the heat source. If required, a thermostat can be incorporated into the circuit

without drawers, it may be easier to attach the tape or cable to the back wall, close to the bottom edge of the cage, and push the cage up to it. In fact, there are very few situations where this system cannot be adopted, and its advantages are that the snake can thermoregulate naturally, it is cheap to install (one cable looped along a rack of shelves can heat up to 100 small boxes if necessary) and cheap to run because the heat produced is being used very efficiently.

An alternative arrangement is to employ long, narrow heat pads, using a separate strip for each shelf. This system has the advantage that some shelves can be heated while others are not (either because they are vacant or because the animals are being cooled down). Strips of heat pad are so thin that they can simply be attached to the surface of the shelf with adhesive tape and without the need to cut a rebate or groove. At the time of writing, heat strips are only available for the European electrical (220-240 volt) system.

Whichever system is used, it is obviously important to ensure that underfloor heating equipment does not create a fire hazard. If necessary, a thin strip of aluminium may be placed over the heat tape or cable and this will help to dissipate the heat as well as to isolate the cages from its source. If in doubt, check with the manufacturers and follow their advice.

Snake-keepers who like to maintain large boas and pythons may have cages large enough to use radiant heat emitters at one end and still have a relatively cool area in the cage. There is nothing wrong with this system, provided there is no danger of the snake coming into contact with the heater and burning itself. However, it is better to use one of the ceramic bulbs which give off heat and no light, since the light-cycle can then be controlled independently if required. A reflector fitted around the heater will help to direct the heat into a limited part of the cage, creating a hot spot.

If a separate room is used to house the collection, it is possible to cut down on individual cage heating by maintaining the whole room at an appropriate temperature. However, from the above remarks it will be obvious that a single temperature will not be satisfactory for all the snakes all the time (to say nothing of the problem of the cages at the top being warmer than those at the bottom). The solution is to compromise by heating the room to a general background temperature of, say, 20°C (68°F) in the summer, and using low-output heat tapes, cables or pads to produce a gradient within each cage.

Kingsnakes (3):
Mexican Kingsnakes

Durango kingsnake,
*Lampropeltis mexicana
greeri*

San Luis Potosí kingsnake,
*Lampropeltis mexicana
mexicana*

Nuevo Leon kingsnake,
*Lampropeltis mexicana
thayeri*. This is the so-
called 'milksnake phase'.
This subspecies occurs in
a variety of other pattern
variations, including a
totally black form

Kingsnakes (4): Mountain Kingsnakes

Arizona mountain kingsnake, *Lampropeltis pyromelana*. This example, from the Chiricahua Mountains, is of the type sometimes known as '*woodini*'

Californian mountain kingsnake, *Lampropeltis zonata pulchra*

HETEROZYGOUS

Heterozygous animals appear normal but carry a recessive gene for some known characteristic, such as albinism or some other colour mutation. The recessive gene is 'hidden' due to the presence of the dominant one, but may be passed on and expressed in future generations. For instance, crossing an animal which is heterozygous for albinism with a pure albino will produce approximately 50 per cent albino and 50 per cent heterozygous offspring (on average). Crossing two heterozygous animals together will produce approximately 25 per cent albino, 50 per cent heterozygous and 25 per cent normal animals (but it will be impossible to distinguish the heterozygous animals from the pure normal animals without doing a series of test-crosses). (See also SELECTIVE BREEDING.)

Note: heterozygous animals are often indicated by the abbreviation 'hetero' on breeders' price-lists.

Chiricahua Mountains, Arizona, the habitat of the Arizona mountain kingsnake and several other interesting species. Snakes from montane regions experience cold winters, even in otherwise hot parts of the world, and should be hibernated if they are to breed.

HIBERNATION

Hibernation is the period of an animal's life when it slows down its metabolism and becomes dormant during cool weather. Since snakes have no means of maintaining their body temperature above that of their surroundings, species living in temperate regions, for instance North America, Europe and southern Africa, must seek out a frost-free and secure place in which to spend the colder months of the year. Depending on their range, they may undergo complete hibernation, in which case they remain totally dormant for several months or, more often, they enter semi-hibernation, during which they may be active off and on throughout the winter when there are warmer spells of weather.

In captivity, temperate and sub-tropical species may all be hibernated. The temperature for these species, e.g. ratsnakes, kingsnakes, garter snakes, etc., should be reduced to about 13-15°C (55-59°F) for two to five months of the winter. Those from more northerly regions, e.g. red-sided garter snakes, or montane habitats, e.g. mountain kingsnakes, may be cooled down even further, to 10-12°C (50-54°F), if required.

The importance of a hibernation period is its influence on the breeding biology of these snakes. Firstly, spermatogenesis, the process by which sperm is formed in the testes of males, only takes place at these low temperatures in some species, so that egg infertility may be a problem in animals which have not been cooled sufficiently during the winter. Secondly, the

period immediately following hibernation is often the time when snakes are most sexually active. Their natural cycles include a period of courtship and mating in the spring, and if both sexes are warmed up at the same time, their reproductive drives will be synchronised. Even tropical species, such as the boas and pythons, appear to require a slightly cooler period if they are to breed regularly. This should not be as extreme as for non-tropical species, however: 20°C (68°F) will suffice in most cases. In a few cases, e.g. indigo snakes and Burmese pythons, mating takes place during cool periods, and it is obviously important to keep pairs or breeding groups together when the temperature is reduced.

The only snakes which need not be hibernated are juveniles, which may be kept warm throughout the winter so that their growth is not interrupted, and pet snakes from which there is no desire to breed. Even so, it will be found that certain species, notably the mountain kingsnakes, fox snakes, etc., will often cease to feed at the end of the summer, irrespective of temperature. This is because their inbuilt biological rhythm is 'expecting' a dormant period and it is difficult to override this, especially in wild-caught adults. If any snake stops feeding in the autumn, provided it is in good condition, the temperature should be reduced, otherwise it will quickly use up all the resources it has stored and lose weight. If kept on a thermal gradient, as recommended (see HEATING), it will be found that many of these 'compulsive hibernators' spend most of their time at the cool end of the cage at this time of the year.

Placing the snakes in hibernation is quite straightforward. After the last feed of the year, they should be kept warm for about two weeks in order to ensure that the gut is empty of all food, then the heat should be removed. If they are kept indoors, it will usually be found that the temperature of an unheated room is approximately correct for non-tropical snakes. Tropical species, and snakes kept outside in a separate building, will probably require some supplementary heating in order to ensure that they do not become too cold. (The opposite problem may occur in warmer regions such as southern California and Florida, where winter temperatures are too warm. Here it may be necessary to use air-conditioning to keep the temperature low enough for some species.) Drinking water should be provided throughout the hibernation period, and the snakes should be inspected at least once every week: if there are any signs of significant weight loss, or wrinkling of the skin, they should be warmed up and fed straightaway.

Otherwise, the temperature can be raised again after two to five months and the snakes will usually resume feeding after a few days. The first two or three meals should be fairly small, in order to allow the digestive system to get back into full swing, and it will often be found that snakes emerging from hibernation shed their skin more or less immediately. Often, individuals which had been problem feeders during the previous year will regain a healthy appetite.

Summary of hibernation temperatures

Montane and northern species (mountain kingsnakes, *Lampropeltis mexicana* subspecies, black ratsnakes, fox snakes, red-sided garter snakes): **10–12°C (50-54°F).**

Other temperate and sub-tropical species (North American and European ratsnakes, common kingsnakes, milksnakes, gopher snakes, hognose snakes, house snakes, rosy boas, etc): **13–15°C (55-59°F).**

Tropical species (most boas and pythons, Asian ratsnakes, etc.): **15–20°C (59-68°F).**

HOGNOSE SNAKES (In colour on pages 50 and 54.)

Three species of hognose snakes are recognised. All are from North America, but two of these nearly always require a diet of frogs or toads and therefore only one, the western hognose snake, *Heterodon nasicus*, is appropriate as a captive. This species grows to about 60 cm (2 ft) in length and is heavy-bodied, bringing to mind the general body shape of a viper. The characteristic which gives them their common name, a bizarre upturned snout, makes them unmistakable. Three subspecies are recognised: *Heterodon nasicus nasicus*, the plains hognose; *Heterodon nasicus gloydi*, the dusty hognose; *Heterodon nasicus kennerlyi*, the Mexican hognose

The plains subspecies has the widest range and is most commonly offered, the dusty hognose is more or less confined to central Texas, and the Mexican hognose is found in southern Texas and northern Mexico. It can be difficult to tell them apart, but a simplified method is as follows. First look at the small scales immediately behind the rostral scale (the one which gives the snake its 'hog' nose). These small scales are irregular in shape and are known as azygous scales. If there are six or less azygous scales, the snake is a Mexican hognose. If there are more than six, count the blotches on the *body*. The dusty hognose has less than 32 (males) or less than 37 (females). If the

A young plains hognose snake, *Heterodon n. nasicus*

blotches total more than these amounts, the snake is a plains hognose. Often, several of the blotches are broken and it may be difficult to decide which to count, but in practice it is not difficult to distinguish between the subspecies at a glance as the markings of *nasicus* are more contrasting than those of the other two, and may be chocolate-brown, reddish or olive in colour. *Gloydi* has more subtle markings and is always tan and brown in colour, whereas *kennerlyi* may be pale grey in colour with darker grey or brown blotches.

All forms inhabit dry regions and prefer areas where the soil is sandy so that they can root out their food using their upturned snouts. They are most active in the evening and early morning, and have two distinct types of defensive behaviour, although captive specimens rarely perform as readily as wild ones. When first disturbed, they will flatten their heads and necks and hiss loudly, and may also make mock strikes to intimidate their enemy. This habit has given them local names such as 'puff adder' and 'hissing adder', despite their harmlessness. If this performance fails to have any effect, the snake may pretend to be dead by rolling over onto its back and allowing its mouth to gape. Unfortunately, the effect is lost if the snake is turned the right way up because it promptly rolls over again!

The care of all forms of western hognose snakes is relatively simple. They require a small cage with a floor covering of wood-shavings or something similar into which they can burrow (soil or sand are not recommended) and a water bowl. Alternatively, they can be kept on newspaper, but in this case they will need a hide-box in which they will spend a large proportion of their time. They invariably feed readily on mice – baby hognose snakes are only about 15-20 cm (6-8 in) in length but will eat newborn mice, whereas adult snakes will take several fully grown mice at each meal. The food is simply picked up and swallowed, often tail first. Strictly speaking, hognose snakes are back-fanged species which can inject a weak form of venom into their prey as they chew on it. They hardly ever bite, however, and, where humans are concerned the venom is not powerful enough to have anything but the slightest local effect.

Hognose snakes mate in the spring, and the eggs are laid about four weeks later. There are also records of autumn matings, with sperm storage then taking place until the following spring. The clutch size varies greatly, from five to 28 eggs, but is usually around ten. As is usual in snakes, bigger females produce bigger clutches. The eggs should be incubated in a moist medium at a temperature of about 28°C (82°F), and they will then hatch in about 60 days. The young grow quickly if adequately fed and are often ready to breed before they reach two years of age. Occasionally, a hatchling will be reluctant to take mice, and pieces of mouse will have to be pushed into its mouth for its first few meals.

HOUSE SNAKES (In colour on page 51.)

The house snakes are all African members of the genus *Lamprophis*. Although a dozen or so species are recognised (including one from the Seychelles), only one is at all commonly available. This is *Lamprophis fuliginosus*, the brown house snake (formerly known as *Boaedon fuliginosus* or *Boaedon lineatus*), which has a wide range covering most of the southern half of Africa. It grows to about 150 cm (5 ft), although specimens of more than 1 m (3 ft) are rare, and is subject to some variation in colour, being pale orange or reddish-brown in some parts of its range and dark brown in others. Its most consistent characteristic is the cream line which runs through each eye, and the pearly lustre on its ventral surface. Some individuals have large, indistinct blotches along the sides, especially on the front portion of the body, but these gradually disappear with age.

Brown house snakes are highly recommended for captivity since they are hardy, invariably eat well and are easy to breed. Even small hatchlings are capable of taking newborn mice and one of the characteristics of this species is its ability to deal with relatively huge prey. Specimens of 50-60 cm (20-24 in) or more can be regarded as sexually mature and they will breed throughout the year if they are kept active. Alternatively, they can be treated like North American or European colubrids and cooled down in the winter, in which case they will breed in the spring or summer. Between eight and ten eggs are laid on average, and these hatch after about 65 days' incubation at 28°C (82°F).

Notes: other species of house snakes, such as *Lamprophis inornatus*, the olive house snake, could be expected to make equally good captives if they were more readily available, while smaller species, such as the very pretty *Lamprophis aurora*, which is bright green with black edges to its scales and an orange vertebral stripe, may be difficult to get started on mice but would prove well worth the effort for more experienced keepers.

HUMIDITY

Humidity is a measure of the amount of moisture in the air, and should not be confused with dampness. Even desert-dwelling snakes require a certain degree of humidity, and species from rain forests or humid lowlands, such as Florida and Louisiana, quickly dehydrate if the atmosphere is excessively dry (this applies especially to hatchlings). In addition, most snakes require more humidity than normal immediately prior to shedding their skin, and may soak in the water bowl for long periods at this time. If the atmosphere inside the cage is too dry, shedding will not take place successfully, as the old skin will become dry and wrinkled. In practice, the air above the water bowl will always contain some moisture and the snake can therefore seek out an area with the appropriate degree of humidity in much the same way as it regulates its temperature, by moving about within the cage.

If the water container is placed at the end of the cage or box furthest from the heat source, this end will be the most humid as well as the coolest, creating a double gradient, and this seems to work quite well for most species. On the other hand, lack of adequate ventilation will increase the humidity, often to unacceptable levels, and care should be taken to ensure that the substrate does not become damp, as this can lead to diseases of the skin.

There are some snakes, however, which require a fairly high humidity at all times, examples being certain of the more arboreal species such as the emerald tree boa, green tree python and the green snakes (*Opheodryas*). These species require regular spraying at all times, but especially when they are getting ready to shed their skins. In addition, certain tropical species, notably some pythons and boas, may also regulate their breeding activities according to the humidity, and these require extra spraying at certain times of the year if they are to breed. Much of this information is still speculative, however, and some experimentation is often necessary.

In general, species requiring higher than normal humidity tend to spend spend little time on the bottom of the cage and it is therefore less important if the substrate becomes damp, although reduced ventilation should not be looked upon as a substitute for regular spraying. Note that the so-called 'water' snakes belonging to the genera *Natrix* and *Nerodia*, and the garter and ribbon snakes (genus *Thamnophis*) do better when kept on a dry substrate and with a low humidity, despite the fact that they are found in damp situations in the wild. They must, of course, have access to a water container at all times, and visits to this seem to satisfy their humidity requirements.

HYBRIDS

Hybrids occur when offspring are produced by crossing two parents which are genetically unlike. Therefore, snakes can be hybrids between subspecies or between species. Offspring from parents of the same species but different subspecies are sometimes called 'intergrades' but this is incorrect: intergrades are animals which come from a region where one subspecies merges into another – they are intermediate between the two subspecies. This is not the same as crossing two animals which may have originated from widely separated geographical areas.

In snakes, different species can often be crossed and the offspring will show some of the characteristics of each parent. Usually these hybrids are between closely related species, e.g. between two kinds of kingsnakes, but it has been shown that hybrids can even occur between parents belonging to different genera, e.g. a gopher snake (genus *Pituophis*) and a ratsnake (genus *Elaphe*). Whether or not this is a desirable trend is left to the individual – some of the resultant offspring are undoubtedly attractive and can make interesting additions to a collection. Unfortunately, they cannot be expected to breed true, and can sometimes produce offspring which look very similar to a totally different species. This leads to the risk that snakes will appear on the market which are of uncertain origin, but which may be sold, either accidentally or intentionally, as rare species.

The very fact that snakes can be hybridised has led to a lack of interest in certain forms because there are known to be impure strains in existence. This is obviously a great shame and breeders are under a moral obligation to 'come clean' over any out-crossing which may have taken place, whether it was between different species or subspecies. Furthermore, breeding pairs of species and subspecies which show wide geographical variation should, if possible, be obtained from the same population (whether or not the populations are recognised as subspecies). A breeder should only resort to crosses between populations and subspecies when a correctly matched partner is not available, as in certain rare and heavily protected species.

HYGIENE

Hygiene comprises keeping the animals, their cages and the room in which they are housed clean and free from sources of infection. It is important in preventing and controlling outbreaks of disease and in taking a pride in the collection – a clean and tidy snake room encourages regular and efficient care of the animals, whereas servicing an untidy room with dirty cages is a chore that will rapidly cause the keeper to lose interest.

Cages should be checked for faeces, uneaten food and shed skins every day. Anything removed from the cages should be taken from the room and disposed of as soon as this task is completed. This procedure need only take a few minutes and will go a long way towards keeping the collection in good order. Every so often, depending on the size and type of cage, the size of the snakes and their diet, each cage should be thoroughly cleaned out by discarding all bedding and wiping or washing the cage itself with a mild disinfectant. The best disinfectant to use is household chlorine bleach, of which a 3-5 per cent solution is usually adequate. Any cage furniture, such as hide-boxes, rocks, bark or branches, should be scrubbed thoroughly and allowed to dry before being replaced. If the cage has been occupied by a diseased snake, these should all be discarded as a matter of course. Water bowls should be thoroughly washed out and refilled with fresh water at least once every week, and more frequently if they become soiled. Every three or four weeks they should be soaked in a 5 per cent bleach solution overnight, then thoroughly rinsed and allowed to dry until all traces of chlorine have dissipated. This should be done routinely irrespective of whether the cage is cleaned.

Bear in mind that any mice, rats or other food animals which are being bred or maintained prior to feeding deserve the same degree of attention as the snakes. Their cages should be cleaned regularly and they should have access to fresh drinking water and food at all times.

The animal room itself should be kept clean and tidy, with no dirty cages or water bowls left lying around. Those of us with old houses realise that snake-rooms can rarely be guaranteed escape-proof, but an uncluttered room will go a long way towards keeping the collection secure. Electrical wiring should be neatly installed and clipped to racks wherever possible and spare equipment should be stored in cupboards or on shelves. Items such as forceps, sexing probes and snake-hooks may be hung on the wall or kept in a drawer where they can be found easily, but any antibiotics or other drugs, whether in use or not, should be housed securely, and locked away if necessary.

I

INBREEDING

Inbreeding occurs when one animal is mated to another to which it is closely related. In many cases this can result in weak or deformed offspring, poor fertility or other undesirable characteristics if it is carried out over several generations. This effect is known as an inbreeding depression and is caused by the accumulation of defective genes in the strain. Some defective genes are probably present in all individuals but are not usually expressed because they are paired with normal genes. When related animals are mated together, however, the chances of the same defective genes coming together are increased.

In the case of snakes, it appears that some species and subspecies are more prone to inbreeding depression than others, and it seems likely that populations which are naturally small, for example those which live in an isolated valley or mountain range, are better able to withstand constant inbreeding (because they are probably inbred naturally and must therefore be free of lethal genes). Other species begin to show signs of inbreeding depression after three or four generations of brother to sister mating and, wherever possible, this system should be avoided. Unfortunately, some species are in such short supply that a certain amount of inbreeding is inevitable. Similarly, if a particular pattern or colour variant is being selected for, it may be necessary to mate related animals in order to increase the numbers of the desired type.

Ideally, matings should be carried out between unrelated individuals if they are available. Where this is not possible, 'new blood' should be introduced to the strain as and when it becomes available, even if this involves using an animal which is not as attractive as those of the original colony. It is often possible to exchange offspring with another breeder who will also welcome the opportunity to introduce fresh blood into his breeding stock (but it is advisable to check that these animals were not obtained from the same source as yours!). Outbreeding (the opposite of inbreeding) to a wild-caught specimen every two or three generations is the most certain way of avoiding inbreeding depression, bearing in mind the precautions necessary when new stock is introduced.

In cases where it is necessary to retain certain genetically determined characteristics, such as the production of albinos, etc., outbreeding with a wild-type animal will make the characteristic 'disappear' temporarily, but it can easily be regained in the next generation by selective breeding (see SELECTIVE BREEDING).

Inbreeding is likely to become an increasingly important aspect of snake-breeding as more and more snakes are bred in captivity. It is therefore important that good breeding records are kept, and, if possible, transferred along with the snakes when they go to new owners, so that effective breeding programmes can be developed which will avoid the problems associated with inbreeding depression.

INCUBATING EGGS

Many of the snakes which are kept and bred in captivity lay eggs, and unless these are incubated in the correct way they will fail to hatch. It is worth making an incubator specifically for the eggs since this is not a difficult or costly task. A cupboard with shelves can often be adapted by the addition of a heater

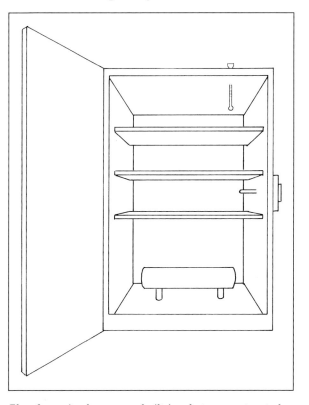

Plan for a simple purpose-built incubator, constructed from wood. The thermostat is mounted on the outside of the unit, with its probe entering through a hole in the back. A heater placed on the bottom provides warmth and a thermometer is suspended through a hole in the top so that the temperature can be monitored without opening the door. It is important to leave gaps at the front and back of each shelf so that warm air can circulate

and thermostat, and by drilling holes to allow electric cable to be admitted. If necessary, the door can be draught-proofed with strips of foam rubber. Conditions inside the incubator must be regulated carefully, and it is essential to set the whole thing up *before* the first eggs appear.

The important variables concerned with incubation are temperature and humidity. A constant temperature is not essential, but will ensure repeatability of results and will make record-keeping simpler. Most temperate species (e.g. rat- and kingsnakes) will hatch successfully if kept at a temperature of 28°C (82°F). This should be maintained by using a reliable thermostat, preferably one which is electronic and designed to operate a low-power heater. This can be mounted outside the cabinet, with its temperature-sensitive probe inside, near the containers of eggs. There must obviously be some means of adjusting the thermostat so that the correct temperature can be set. The heater itself may be of any type, including a heat tape

A clutch of snake eggs, arranged in a plastic box half-filled with vermiculite. This should be labelled to give details of the species, number of eggs contained and the date they were laid

wrapped around a board, a heat pad or a small ceramic heater, but it is important that it is not too powerful otherwise the thermostat will be unable to even out fluctuations efficiently. Careful thought should be given to the siting of the heater in order to ensure that the temperature is evenly distributed throughout the incubator. One way of doing this is to place it at the bottom of the cabinet and towards the back. The shelves on which the containers of eggs will rest are then arranged so that there is a small gap at the back and at the front. Warm air will circulate around the cabinet by convection. Alternatively, a small fan may be installed (as in some modern ovens) to distribute the warm air.

Snake eggs are covered with a permeable shell which allows water and air to move through it. If they are kept too dry, water will pass out of the egg and it will desiccate. If they are kept too wet, air will be unable to enter and the embryo will suffocate. The most effective method of ensuring the correct conditions is to rest the eggs on a substrate which can be kept moist throughout the incubation period. Vermiculite is a very satisfactory substrate, but others, such as perlite, sand and sawdust, have also been used successfully. Water is added to the substrate until it is thoroughly moist and there is no free water remaining (with vermiculite, two parts of vermiculite to one part of water, by volume, is often about right, but the exact proportions depend on the grade of vermiculite being used). Once the substrate has been put in a container such as a lunch-box and has been evenly moistened, the eggs can be placed in small depressions made with a finger. If the eggs are firmly stuck together (which they often will be unless they are discovered within a few hours of being laid), no attempt should be made to separate them, and the clump should be laid in a single large depression in the substrate, with as many eggs

'De Luxe' incubator used by Steve Thomas of California. The heater is placed beneath a false floor and the warm air travels up two plastic tubes in the back corners. Wire shelves allow good air circulation and there is a glass inspection panel in the door. A drawer and cupboard below the main compartment provide storage for assorted snake-keeping paraphernalia

Where eggs stick together after laying, no attempt should be made to separate them

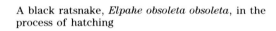

A black ratsnake, *Elpahe obsoleta obsoleta*, in the process of hatching

as possible in contact with it. (Provided the atmosphere in the container is humid, all the eggs will hatch, irrespective of whether they are in contact with the substrate or not.) The lid, which should be a fairly tight fit, is now replaced on the container and the whole box placed in the incubator. The air in the container will be sufficient to supply the developing embryos, and will in any case be renewed every time the eggs are inspected.

Many clutches contain infertile eggs and these can be identified by their yellowish colour, compared to the pure white to pinkish colour of good eggs. It is not essential to discard these infertile eggs, especially if they are stuck to good ones. Mould will soon develop on them and they will shrivel away, but fertile eggs are well protected against mould and will continue to develop even if their surface becomes discoloured. If more than one or two eggs are infertile, or if the female persistently lays clutches of infertile eggs, the fault usually lies with the male. Very often, males are not cooled down sufficiently and although they may develop some sperm, this will not be viable.

Towards the end of incubation (60-70 days in many cases) the eggs will start to look misshapen as the young snake is formed. Eventually, small slits will appear in the shell and the hatchling will emerge, sometimes several days after it first slits the shell. It is a mistake to be in too much of a hurry to remove the hatchlings from their container since they will not be ready to feed until after they have shed their skin for the first time, usually in about four days, and the warm moist environment of the incubator seems to benefit them. Often, the whole clutch will not hatch together and hatchlings may emerge over a four- or five-day period – this is perfectly normal and unhatched eggs should not be opened artificially until there is no hope of them hatching on their own. They will usually be found to contain partially developed but dead young, which are sometimes deformed. A high failure rate of this type may be due to several causes including highly inbred parents (see INBREEDING), incorrect incubation conditions or stress in the female before laying. (**In colour on page 54.**)

INDIGO SNAKE (In colour on page 51.)

The indigo snake, *Drymarchon corais*, is one of the more desirable species. Specimens from the Florida subspecies *D. c. couperi* are jet black in colour with large shiny scales. The chin may be deep pink or grey. This form should not be confused with South and Central American subspecies of the 'indigo snake', which are more properly known as cribos, and which make unsatisfactory captives.

Florida indigos are large docile creatures growing to 2 m (6½ ft) or more. Their slender bodies are beautifully iridescent and they tend to be more active than most of the colubrids which are available, being closely related to the diurnal whipsnakes and racers. They therefore require very large cages, which should contain a hide-box. A substrate of newspaper, wood shavings or compressed sawdust pellets is recommended, because this species can be messy. Although they usually eat mice and rats, some individuals prefer fish or frogs, especially when young. Indigo snakes are happy to eat other snakes too, and so must be kept separately. They require a temperature of 25-30°C (77-86°F), which should be allowed to fall to about 15°C (59°F) during the winter, which is their mating season.

Breeding is by no means easy, and there is no certain method which will lead to success. Vitamin deficiencies have been suggested as a reason for failure to breed and experiments have been carried out using dietary supplements and special ultra-violet lighting, but the results are inconclusive. Males may fight amongst themselves during the breeding season, and females are also likely to be bitten and scarred at this time. After mating, the females may retain the sperm for many weeks, before eventually laying up to 20 eggs. A high rate of infertility (often 100 per cent) is one of the problems which have plagued breeders. Good eggs hatch after a variable incubation period of 70-100 days and the young are 50-60 cm (20-24 in) in length. Some will take young mice straightaway; others require fish or frogs, or their food should be scented with these items.

Indigo snakes are protected throughout their range and the opportunities to purchase even captive-bred individuals are strictly limited. This, together with their desirability, has led to high prices.

K

KINGSNAKES

The kingsnakes and their close relatives, the milksnakes (dealt with under a separate heading), are exclusively American colubrids, ranging from Canada down into Ecuador. At least seven species are recognised in total, of which several are divided into a number of distinct subspecies. The main species groups are as follows:

- [ ] Prairie kingsnake, *Lampropeltis calligaster*
- [ ] Common kingsnake, *Lampropeltis getulus*
- [ ] Mexican kingsnake, *Lampropeltis mexicana, alterna*
- [ ] Mountain kingsnakes, *Lampropeltis pyromelana, ruthveni* and *zonata*
- [ ] Milksnake, *Lampropeltis triangulum*

As a group, these are among the most popular species with snake-keepers. They are all attractive snakes with smooth shiny scales, many of them brightly coloured. Their care and breeding is usually straightforward, although some species are easier and therefore more suitable for beginners, than others.

In general, kingsnakes should be kept in small to medium-sized cages or boxes with the minimum of furnishings. As they tend to be secretive by nature, a hide-box or drawer is essential, otherwise they have no special requirements. All species will eat mice, although some are by nature lizard- and snake-

eaters, and hatchlings of these species sometimes require their food to be scented with a lizard before it is acceptable. Because they are sometimes cannibalistic, individuals are best kept separately, except when breeding. Nor is it possible to keep different species of kingsnakes together.

Summer temperatures of around 25-30°C (77-86°F) are required, although kingsnakes are not delicate species and occasional temperature drops will do no harm. The provision of a thermal gradient (see TEMPERATURE) is essential. They should be cooled down during the winter, especially if breeding is to be attempted: threshold winter temperatures vary from species to species, but montane kingsnakes, including the *L. mexicana* group, require at least two months at 13°C (55°F) or less if they are to produce fertile eggs. Lowland species appear to be able to breed successfully after a less severe temperature drop, but 15°C (59°F) should be aimed for.

Lampropeltis alterna – Grey-banded Kingsnake (In colour on page 55.)

The grey-banded kingsnake is found in southern Texas and northern Mexico and is sometimes classified with the Mexican kingsnake as *Lampropeltis mexicana alterna*. It grows to a little under 1 m (3 ft) in length and occurs in a bewildering variety of colour forms, with hardly any two snakes being alike. Basically, two distinct phases can be distinguished. 'Blair's phase' snakes have broad bands: these may be pale grey and orange, dark grey and orange or pale grey and dark grey. In each case these broad bands are separated by narrow black bands which may be thinly edged in white. 'Alterna phase' snakes are pale grey with narrow black bands, sometimes containing a small amount of orange in their centres. Secondary thin black bands, often broken, usually alternate with the more definite primary dark bands.

Care and breeding are as for other kingsnakes. This is a secretive species which must have the security of a hide-box or a drawer. About ten eggs are laid and these hatch in about 65 days when incubated at a temperature of 28°C (82°F). The hatchlings are lizard-eaters by inclination and it may require some effort to induce them to eat newborn mice at first. Once they get started they generally thrive and grow rapidly, attaining breeding age in two years. However, males must be cooled down in the winter if fertile eggs are to be obtained.

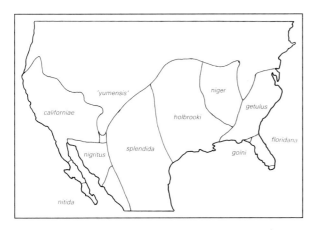

Distribution of the various subspecies of the common kingsnake, *Lampropeltis getulus*, in North America. The locations of the forms *brooksi, nitida* and *yumensis* are also shown, although these are not always recognised as subspecies

The very popular Blair's phase of the grey-banded kingsnake

Lampropeltis calligaster – Prairie and Mole Kingsnakes
Two subspecies are recognised:

Lampropeltis calligaster calligaster – Prairie Kingsnake (**In colour on page 55.**)
This subspecies is found in the eastern USA and averages about 1 m (3 ft) in length. It is pale brown in colour with a series of rich brown or reddish-brown blotches along the back.

Care and breeding are as for other members of the genus. The prairie kingsnake, although less spectacularly coloured than some of the other members of its genus, is a tough, well-mannered species which breeds freely. Clutches of 5-16 eggs are laid about four to six weeks after mating, and these hatch after an incubation period of about 60 days (at 28°C/82°F). The young measure about 30 cm (1 ft) in length and will readily feed on baby mice. Females in good condition will usually produce a second clutch during the summer if required.

An amelanistic strain is available. The adults are handsome, bone-coloured animals with faint traces of the dorsal markings, whereas the hatchlings have bright-red body blotches. Neither adults not juveniles have the rather sickly appearance of certain other amelanistic strains. (**In colour on page 18.**)

Lampropeltis calligaster rhombomaculata – Mole Kingsnake
The mole kingsnake is found further west than the prairie kingsnake, and is darker in colour, sometimes reddish-brown. In adults especially, the ground colour becomes so dark that the dorsal blotches are sometimes difficult to discern.

Care and breeding are as for *L. c. calligaster*. This subspecies is not as frequently available.

Lampropeltis getulus – **Common Kingsnake**
Among the largest and most impressive snakes of the genus *Lampropeltis*, adults of this species may reach almost 2 m (6½ ft) although the average is closer to 1 m (3 ft). There is great variation among the subspecies, which are described separately, but most forms are attractively marked in black (or dark brown) and white (or yellow). The various forms of the common kingsnake are ideal subjects for beginners as well as more experienced snake-keepers. All are easy to breed and rear, and the majority settle down well and become tame.

Their general care is as described for the genus, and breeding can be expected from individuals of two or more years old, by which time they should be approaching 1 m (3 ft) in length. The number of eggs in a clutch varies somewhat among the subspecies, but most will produce two, and sometimes more, clutches during each breeding season if they are in good condition. Although they should be cooled down during the winter, it appears that a very low temperature is not essential for successful fertilisation of the eggs.

Up to eleven subspecies are recognised, all of which are occasionally kept in captivity, although some are far more popular than others.

Lampropeltis getulus brooksi – South Florida Kingsnake
This is similar to the more familiar Florida kingsnake (below), but more heavily marked with yellow. It is a variable subspecies and some strains are more attractive than others.

Care and breeding are as described for *L. g. floridana* (see below). This snake is one of the less common forms.

Lampropeltis getulus californiae – Californian Kingsnake (**In colour on page 58.**)
This subspecies is found over much of the American south west and is highly variable. Apart from the two distinct pattern types described below, the colours of both the background and the markings may vary. The most widespread phase is a black or brown snake with 21-44 white, cream or yellow bands, or rings, around its body. Examples from the coastal part of the range tend to be brown and cream or brown and yellow, while desert examples are closer to jet black and pure white. The number of bands also varies, with animals from the Mojave Desert region having the highest number on average. Good desert examples are rare in the wild and therefore highly sought after. A striped form is found only in and around San Diego county. In these examples, the colours are as described but the white or cream areas are confined to three stripes, one along the dorsal mid-line and one on each of the flanks. Both the striped and banded varieties may occasionally have solid black undersides.

Care and breeding are as described for the genus. Californian kingsnakes usually lay fairly small clutches of 4-12 large eggs. These hatch after about 60 days at 28°C (82°F). Matings between striped and banded individuals usually result in offspring which have intermediate markings, i.e. traces of bands and stripes. These

Leonis phase of the Nuevo Leon kingsnake, *Lampropeltis mexicana thayeri*

are variously known as aberrant or dot-dash kingsnakes. Hatchlings measure about 30 cm (1 ft) in length and usually take baby mice readily, although the black-and-white desert strains can occasionally be somewhat reluctant to start feeding.

Variations: apart from the aberrant-patterned type mentioned, albino strains of both the striped and banded forms are available.

Lampropeltis getulus floridana – Florida Kingsnake

Florida kingsnakes are brown with cream or yellow centres to their scales. The markings are not evenly distributed, however, and scales with large pale spots are arranged into a series of crossbars linking pale-centred scales on each flank. The remaining scales are only faintly spotted and tend to form darker blotches along the back of the snake. Young examples often have red or pink markings among the pale-centred scales, but these invariably fade with age.

Care and breeding are as described for the genus. Florida kingsnakes are one of the larger subspecies and often have large clutches of up to 20 small eggs. The young are especially voracious and have cannibalistic tendencies, so on no account should they be kept together. Like other eastern subspecies, they are less able to tolerate dry conditions, especially as hatchlings, and should not be left without water for any length of time.

Lampropeltis getulus 'yumensis' – Yuma Kingsnake (**In colour on page 58.**)

This snake is found around the southern Arizona/California border region. It is probably not a valid subspecies, but rather an intergrade between *L. g. californiae* and *L. g. nigritus*, or *L. g. californiae* and *L. g. splendida*. It is a black-and-white banded kingsnake in which the very narrow white bands are formed with scales which have brown bases.

Care and breeding are as described for the genus.

Lampropeltis getulus getulus – Chain Kingsnake, Eastern Kingsnake

The chain kingsnake is found in the eastern states of the USA, except for Florida. It is black or brown in colour with narrow, paler cross bands. The bands fork into two on the flanks and each arm joins up with one of the arms of the adjacent bands.

Care and breeding are as described for the genus. This is a large subspecies which may lay up to 20 rather small eggs. The remarks pertaining to the hatchlings of the Florida kingsnake also apply to this subspecies.

Lampropeltis getulus goini – Blotched Kingsnake (**In colour on page 58.**)

A very restricted subspecies whose range is limited to a small area of northern Florida in the region of the Apalachicola valley. The most variable form of the common kingsnake – hardly any two are the same! The basic colour is formed of scales which are half black and half white. On this may be superimposed a series of large or small blotches along the back. Other individuals have a single dark stripe running down the centre of the back, while a few are without any overlying pattern whatsoever. There is a strong tendency toward pink or red scales along the flanks, especially in hatchlings.

Care and breeding are as described for the genus.

Lampropeltis getulus holbrooki – Speckled Kingsnake (**In colour on page 59.**)
The speckled kingsnake is an eastern subspecies, found from the Gulf coast north into the central states. Good examples, i.e. from the centre of the range, are black with an even speckling of white or yellow spots, one on each scale. This subspecies intergrades with several of the neighbouring forms, and pure *holbrooki* are sometimes difficult to obtain. This subspecies has a reputation for being aggressive, although captive-raised individuals are easily handled.

Care and breeding are as described for the genus. Speckled kingsnakes have large clutches of up to 20 small eggs. The hatchlings are smaller than those of most other subspecies, on average, but they are good feeders and grow rapidly. An albino strain is widely available.

Lampropeltis getulus niger – Black Kingsnake
Found in north-eastern USA, the black kingsnake is like a dark version of the chain kingsnake, in which the markings are all but obscured.

Care and breeding are as described for the genus. It is not so often kept in captivity, as the Mexican black kingsnake (see below) is generally a more attractive subspecies.

The banded form of the Californian kingsnake, *Lampropeltis g. californiae*, is deservedly one of the most popular snakes with beginners and experts alike

Lampropeltis getulus nigritus – Mexican Black
Kingsnake (**In colour on page 59.**)
Found in the arid parts of north-west Mexico,
this subspecies is, strictly speaking, a pure jet-
black kingsnake, in which form it is one of the
most impressive subspecies. Many strains
produce hatchlings which have traces of *L. g.
splendida* markings, although these should
gradually disappear with age.

Care and breeding are as described for the
genus. Small clutches of 6-12 large eggs are laid.

Lampropeltis getulus 'nitida' – Baja Kingsnake
Found only in the Cape region of Baja
California, this is rather like an indistinctly
marked, banded Californian kingsnake, only
not as attractive. It is probably not a valid
subspecies, and is mainly of interest to the
specialist.

Care and breeding, as far as is known, are as
described for the genus.

Lampropeltis getulus splendida – Desert
Kingsnake (**In colour on page 59.**)
This kingsnake comes from the desert regions
of Arizona, New Mexico, South Texas and
northern Mexico. The ground colour is jet-black
in this subspecies, the flanks are heavily

Arizona mountain kingsnake, *Lampropeltis
pyromelana*, devouring a mouse

marked with white or yellow scales, and the
back is crossed by a series of narrow white or
yellow bands. In other words, it is a speckled
kingsnake with a series of solid black blotches
along its back. This subspecies intergrades with
L. g. holbrooki and *L. g. nigritus*, and pure
examples may be hard to find.

Care and breeding are as described for the
genus. Small clutches of 6-12 large eggs are laid.

Lampropeltis mexicana – Mexican Kingsnake

Three, or possibly four, subspecies of this highly
variable kingsnake have been described. They
grow to about 1 m (3 ft) in length and are found
in mountainous parts of south Texas and
adjoining northern Mexico, where they have
somewhat restricted ranges. The great amount
of variation within the subspecies provides
ample scope for the specialist breeder, but some
forms are rather difficult to care for, especially
when it comes to raising the hatchlings, which

may be reluctant to take baby mice unless they are scented with a lizard. Even then, the odd individual will require force-feeding.

In other respects, their care is as for the genus. However, in these montane snakes a cooling down period in the winter, to 13°C (55°F) or less, is absolutely essential if they are to produce fertile eggs. This applies particularly to *L. m. greeri* and *L. m. thayeri*. All are capable of breeding at two years of age if well fed, and it is possible to obtain two clutches per season from each female. Three subspecies are dealt with here – for *L. m. alterna* see under *Lampropeltis alterna*.

Lampropeltis mexicana greeri – Durango Kingsnake (**In colour on page 62.**)
This snake is pale grey, cream or buff in colour with bands of red, each bordered by black. The width of the bands is variable, and they may consist merely of narrow black saddles with only the faintest trace of red in their centre.

Care and breeding are as described for the species. Note the remarks concerning a winter cooling off period. This subspecies lays about six eggs which hatch in just over 60 days at 28°C (82°F). The hatchlings measure about 25 cm (10 in), but have narrow heads and can only manage small baby mice. Some may be reluctant to start feeding without manipulating the odour of the food.

Lampropeltis mexicana mexicana – San Luis Potosi Kingsnake (**In colour on page 62.**)
Less variable than the other subspecies, San Luis Potosi kingsnakes are grey in colour with saddles of rich red or reddish-brown, each narrowly bordered by black. An intricate red marking, of variable shape, is usually present on the top of the head.

Care and breeding are as described for the species, although this is a far less finicky form than the other subspecies. It usually feeds well from the start and produces larger clutches, of 9-15 eggs.

Lampropeltis mexicana thayeri – Nuevo Leon Kingsnake (**In colour on page 62.**)
This is an extremely variable subspecies. Three distinct colour phases may be identified: the 'milksnake' phase, in which red and grey bands of nearly equal width are separated by narrow black borders; the 'leonis' phase, in which the pale grey or fawn background is marked with narrow red saddles with black edges; and the melanistic phase, in which the animal is totally black. Individuals may also be intermediate between the milksnake and leonis phases, and this whole spectrum of possibilities may be produced from a single clutch!

Care and breeding are as described for the species. This form is more like *greeri* in its general appearance and behaviour and the comments regarding that subspecies apply here also, although the general impression is that *thayeri* is slightly easier to care for.

***Lampropeltis pyromelana* – Arizona Mountain Kingsnake (In colour on page 63.)**
This is a specialised montane snake, found only in a few isolated mountain ranges in Arizona, Utah, Nevada and New Mexico, and in adjacent parts of Mexico. It is a slender tri-coloured kingsnake with a clear orange-red ground colour broken by triads of black-white-black bands, and with a white snout. There is variation in the extent of the black bands and a number of subspecific forms have been named, but these names are not consistently applied and may not be valid. In general, *L. p. pyromelana* is a form in which the red areas are complete, i.e. not broken along the dorsal line by black, whereas *L. p. woodini* has many triads in which the black divides the red into two wedge-shaped areas on the flanks. Intermediate stages are frequently seen. A third subspecies, *L. p. knoblocki*, in which the white bands expand on the flanks, has been described from Mexico. *L. p. infralabialis* is a rare subspecies from Utah.

General care and breeding are as described for the genus. This is a secretive species which, in the wild, is forced into hibernation for many months due to a cold montane climate. In captivity, it often refuses to feed after the summer and must be cooled down. In any case, failure to do this will result in infertile eggs. Young snakes may remain active throughout the winter, and thus grow more quickly, but it is unusual for this species to reach sexual maturity in less than three years.

Females produce small clutches, averaging three to six elongated eggs. These hatch after about 65 days at 28°C (82°F) and the hatchlings measure about 25 cm (10 in). They normally take newborn mice, but occasionally require these to be scented with a lizard at first. They often prefer to feed in a confined space, such as a small hide-box, and failure to feed can often be caused by housing them in a large cage with no suitable retreat. Due to their short period of activity, it is rare for a female to produce a second clutch during the breeding season. However, this is compensated for by their long lifespan, some individuals continuing to breed until they are 15 years of age or more.

Lampropeltis ruthveni – Queretaro Mountain Kingsnake

This is a small mountain kingsnake from Mexico, usually less than 1 m (3 ft) in length and with bands of red, white and black circling its body. The white bands often become grey as the animals mature, and the snout is invariably black.

Care and breeding are as described for the genus. This is an especially hardy little kingsnake, which adapts well to captivity.

Females of two years or more lay clutches of six to ten eggs which hatch after about 60 days at 28°C (82°F). The hatchlings measure 25–30 cm (10–12 in) and usually feed readily on newborn mice. Two or more clutches can be laid each season if the female is in good condition.

Note that this species appears to be capable of cross-breeding with practically any other species of king- or milksnake, producing a selection of weird and not-so-wonderful

Lampropeltis zonata – **Californian Mountain Kingsnake (In colour on page 63.)**
This is a small, brightly coloured mountain kingsnake, from isolated mountain ranges in California, Oregon, Washington and Baja California. It has bright red, white and black bands and the snout is always black. It is possibly the prettiest of all the tri-coloured snakes. At least six subspecies are recognised, but differences among them are slight and accurate identification can only be made if their origin is known.

Care and breeding are as described for the genus, but *L. zonata* is not among the easiest of kingsnakes to keep. In particular, the small hatchlings are often reluctant to feed on mice, and some individuals are never really happy on a diet of rodents. Like the Arizona mountain kingsnake, this species normally hibernates for several months in the winter, and captives may refuse to feed during the colder months, even though their cages are artificially heated.

Females produce one clutch, of about six eggs, each year. These hatch after about 60 days' incubation at 28°C (82°F), and the young require small lizards or lizard-scented mice. The development of a strain which feeds readily on mice would be a most useful and much needed breeding project to undertake. The subspecies from Baja California, *L. z. algama*, is said to produce larger young than the others and to be a more aggressive feeder, although it, too, can be difficult and is, in any case, rarely available.

The Californian mountain kingsnake, *Lampropeltis zonata*, can be distinguished from the Arizona mountain kingsnake by its jet black snout

hybrids. Furthermore, its taxonomy is rather uncertain at present and it may well be reclassified at some stage in the future.

Milksnakes

Mexican milksnake,
*Lampropeltis triangulum
annulata*

Pueblan milksnake,
*Lampropeltis triangulum
campbelli*

Honduran milksnake,
*Lampropeltis triangulum
hondurensis*

Sinaloan milksnake,
*Lampropeltis triangulum
sinaloae*

L

THE LAW

Snake-keeping is governed by a variety of laws. Obviously, these vary from country to country and, in the USA, from state to state. Furthermore, many of them are continually revised or supplemented. Persons hoping to keep snakes should check that they are legally entitled to do so and that the species they wish to keep are not in any way restricted before going ahead with any further arrangements. Laws pertaining to snake-keeping generally fall into three categories: conservation, public safety and miscellaneous legal restrictions.

Conservation

Many snakes are protected in their countries of origin, in which case their movements may well be controlled by the Convention on International Trade in Endangered Species of Flora and Fauna (CITES). Very rare species, listed below, are placed in Appendix I of the CITES lists and can only be bought, sold or maintained if an exemption has been obtained. Many other species are placed in Appendix II and may be kept legally but not imported or exported without the appropriate licences. In

the USA, restrictions extend to interstate movements in some cases (e.g. indigo snakes), where they are covered by the 'Lacey' Act. In addition, many countries give outright or partial protection to local species, and this is usually the case for any species living within areas designated as national parks, etc. Flaunting of these laws not only gives reptile-keepers a bad name, but is contrary to the spirit of snake-keeping and breeding.

Species of snakes listed in Appendix I by CITES may not be held in captivity without an exemption (which is rarely granted to private individuals except under certain circumstances, e.g. if the animals were captive-bred). At present, this list comprises the following species.

Acrantophis dumerilii Dumeril's ground boa
Acrantophis madagascariensis Madagascan
 ground boa
Bolyeria multicarinata Round Island boa
Casarea dussumieri Round Island boa
Epicrates monensis Mona Island boa
Epicrates inornatus Puerto Rican boa
Epicrates subflavus Jamaican boa
Python molurus molurus Indian python
Sanzinia madagascariensis Madagascan
 tree boa

Appendix 1 species, such as this Dumeril's ground boa, *Acranthopis dumerilii*, can only be kept in captivity if a CITES exemption is granted.

Public safety

There are often regulations governing the keeping of dangerous snakes. These may be national or local laws and are designed to protect the general public from dangerous pets. Species involved include the vipers and cobras, certain back-fanged species and, in some cases, large boas and pythons. Certain small-minded authorities enforce a complete ban on the keeping of any snakes within the area of their jurisdiction.

Miscellaneous legal restrictions

Various authorities restrict the keeping of snakes for public display, for sale or for other commercial activities, or the release of exotic species into the wild. These restrictions are unlikely to affect amateur snake-keepers.

Aside from the above specific legal requirements, snake-keepers are under a moral obligation not to make their hobby objectionable to the public at large. Bear in mind that many people are not fond of snakes and, unreasonable though this may seem, their opinions should be respected. Care should be taken to ensure that snakes do not escape, especially in residential areas, and animals should not be draped around the neck and taken into the local pub, or whatever. If snake-keeping is to be regarded as an acceptable pursuit, then every effort should be made to educate and reassure neighbours and friends.

LIFE-SPAN

The age to which snakes can survive under wild conditions is virtually unknown. In captivity, their natural life-spans are probably exceeded in many cases, given the fact that they are protected against diseases, parasites and predators, and that they have access to a more predictable food supply.

Most colubrid species, such as kingsnakes and ratsnakes, will live for twelve to fifteen years or more in captivity, and breed right up until the end of their lives. Species with a more active lifestyle, such as garter snakes and racers, probably fall slightly short of these ages, on average, whereas larger snakes, such as the pythons and boas, can exceed them comfortably.

Most medium-sized snakes can reach sexual maturity by the time they are two years of age if they are fed well while they are young. Others take three or more years, especially if they are larger or if they go through periods of hibernation, during which their growth will obviously be arrested. Sexual maturity is reached when snakes are approximately half-grown. Unlike birds and mammals, snakes have an indeterminate growth pattern. This means that they can continue to grow throughout their lives, although their growth rate slows down with age.

LIGHTING

The general rule, when lighting snake cages, is that the lighting should be subdued. Snakes are secretive by nature and will be placed under stress if they are kept in a brightly lit environment. Most of the commonly kept types are nocturnal or active during the evening and early morning anyway, and if the purpose of the lighting is to make them show themselves off, then this will be counter-productive since they will spend the entire day in their hide-box. Cages which are placed in a room which receives some indirect natural light should not require separate lights at all. If the cages are kept in a dark room, then the room should be lit, preferably with fluorescent tubes, and these can be controlled by a time-switch so that the snakes have a reasonably natural day-night cycle.

There are only two exceptions to this rule. Firstly, snakes which like to bask, mainly diurnal species from cooler climates, such as the garter snakes (*Thamnophis*), indigo snake (*Drymarchon corais*), racers and whipsnakes (*Coluber* and *Masticophis*) may gain some psychological benefits from lying beneath a light source. This can be a light bulb, which will also give off some heat, or it can be a fluorescent tube, in which case heat should be provided by an underfloor system as described under HEATING. Although there is no conclusive evidence at present, some species which like to bask may benefit from a natural spectrum tube.

The other exception is in the case of planted vivaria, discussed under the heading CAGE FURNISHINGS. Here, it is the plants that require light of suitable intensity and colour. Horticultural suppliers can probably give the best advice on these matters but, in general, a medium-sized cage will require two natural spectrum tubes of the appropriate length and these should be suspended about 30 cm (1 ft) above the plants. The snakes in such a cage must have an opportunity to shelter from the light.

Asian Pythons

Blood python, *Python curtus*, a short, stout python from South-East Asia

Burmese python, *Python molurus bivittatus*, a large python which breeds readily in captivity

An albino form of the Burmese python, now being widely bred in captivity

Although most snakes kept in captivity lay eggs, some, such as this American water snake, *Nerodia cyclopion*, and the boas, are live-bearing

LIVE-BEARING SNAKES

Although most snakes which are likely to be kept in captivity are egg-layers, a few give birth to living young. These are, in the main, the garter snakes (*Thamnophis*), North American water snakes (*Nerodia*) and the boas.

There is usually no need to make special arrangements for the birth of these species, but it is sometimes helpful if a box of moist sphagnum moss is placed in the cage, since the young are often covered with mucus at first and bedding such as wood-shavings and newspaper is inclined to stick to them. One precaution which must be taken is to ensure that there are no small cracks through which the newborn snakes can crawl – it is easy to become complacent over the security of a cage in which a large adult is housed, and overlook places where wood has warped or the lid does not fit too well. Rearing the newborn snakes is the same as for those which hatch from eggs (see HATCHLINGS and FEEDING HATCHLINGS).

LYRE SNAKES (In colour on page 51.)

Snakes of the genus *Trimorphodon* are known as lyre snakes because of a lyre-shaped marking on the top of their head. Two species are recognised, of which *T. tau* from Mexico is not readily available, and the other, *T. biscutatus*, which has a more northern distribution, only rarely so. The latter occurs in a number of subspecies.

These are rear-fanged snakes which are harmless to humans. (*T. biscutatus* can be aggressive in temperament, but eventually calms down in captivity.) They require warm dry conditions and are active mainly at night. Adults will eat mice, but hatchlings would probably require lizards at first. This is not a popular species among snake-keepers.

M

MELANISTIC SNAKES

Melanistic animals are those in which there is an excess of black pigment. This may vary from a tendency to become darker with age, e.g. in some of the milksnakes, to animals which are totally black throughout their lives. It occurs as a mutation in individuals but, in some circumstances, may be advantageous and therefore spreads naturally throughout a population. An example of this is the population of melanistic common garter snakes which is found around Lake Erie in North America. Melanistic snakes absorb radiation more efficiently and are more likely to thrive in cold environments. Where there is a geographic variation within a species, it is often the populations at the colder extremes of the range which tend towards melanism, for instance black pine snakes and black ratsnakes. Genes for melanism are often dominant (see GENETICS).

Several species tend towards melanism in parts of their range. This is the black pine snake, *Pituophis melanoleucus lodingi*

MILKSNAKES

Members of the species *Lampropeltis triangulum* are known collectively as milksnakes. The species exists in a huge variety of forms and at least 25 subspecies are recognised by some authorities. Their typical coloration is of red, white and black rings encircling the body. The number of these sets of rings, or triads, is diagnostic in separating the subspecies. Owing to their bright colours, many snake-keepers specialise in milksnakes and very many are bred in captivity. The suitability of the various types depends largely on diet: hatchlings of several of the smaller forms are tiny and therefore difficult to get started on baby mice. However, there is still plenty of scope within this species and the forms described are all suitable and recommended.

The care of milksnakes is as for typical colubrids. They require medium-sized cages or boxes and a summer temperature of around 25°C (77°F). They are secretive and require a hide-box if kept in a large cage, or they may be kept in a cage with a false bottom and a drawer. They can be fed on mice, starting with newborn mice in the case of hatchlings. Hatchlings of some subspecies may be reluctant to take rodents at first and it may be necessary to transfer the scent of a lizard onto the mouse. Alternatively, the snake should be placed in a small tub with a newborn mouse – this will often encourage it to start feeding. In extreme

Australasian Pythons

Children's python, *Liasis childreni*, a small Australian species which can be cared for in the same way as a kingsnake or ratsnake

Stimson's python, *Liasis stimsoni*, has only recently been recognised as a separate species. It is even smaller than the Children's python, and paler in colour

The diamond python, *Morelia spilotes spilotes*, is possibly Australia's most spectacular python, but is bred in limited numbers

D'Albertis' python, *Liasis albertisi*, from New Guinea

Distribution of the subspecies of milksnakes *Lampropeltis triangulum* in North, Central and South America. It is important to note that some subspecies merge into others where their ranges meet, and intermediate individuals, or intergrades, many not fit textbook descriptions exactly

cases it may be necessary to push small pieces of mouse into its mouth for the first few meals (see also FEEDING HATCHLINGS).

Breeding is usually straightforward. Milksnakes mature in their second or third year, and should be cooled down during the winter prior to mating. Males and females are put together in the spring and mating normally takes place within a week or two. The eggs are laid about one month later. The clutch size depends, to some extent, on subspecies. Provided the female is in good condition, she can often be remated for a second clutch. The gestation period for the second clutch is usually slightly shorter than for the first. The incubation period for the eggs is usually 60-65 days at 28°C (82°F).

Although the distribution map shows the approximate locations of all the subspecies currently recognised, only the most distinctive and those generally available are considered below. Although new subspecies are becoming available constantly, through the efforts of breeders, the following list should include all of those which are likely to be offered for sale at anything short of a king's ransom. Some special requirements are noted under the appropriate headings, otherwise care is as detailed above.

Lampropeltis triangulum annulata – Mexican Milksnake (**In colour on page 82.**)
Despite its common name, this species is also found over a large portion of southern Texas. The ground colour is rich deep red or maroon and the pale bands vary from pure white through to bright yellow or gold. The snout is shiny black. Although there is a tendency for members of this subspecies to darken with age, this is not as pronounced as in some of the other forms. This is a small subspecies, maturing at about 60 cm (2 ft) in total length, and is of a calm disposition (again differing from several of the other forms).

Care and breeding are relatively easy. Although the adults are small, the hatchlings are relatively large, about 25 cm (10 in), and usually accept newborn mice without trouble. They grow quickly and will breed at two years of age. Females lay one or more clutches of around six to ten eggs each year and these hatch after about 60 days at 28°C (82°F).

Lampropeltis triangulum arcifera – Jalisco Milksnake
Jalisco milksnakes, which come from the region of Mexico with the same name, are medium sized, growing to about 1 m (3 ft), and tend to remain more brightly coloured than many of the other forms. The triads are close together and the red is clear and bright.

Care and breeding are as for other milksnakes. The hatchlings are relatively small, but are usually reared without problems. This form is not as readily available at present as several of the others.

Lampropeltis triangulum campbelli – Pueblan Milksnake (**In colour on page 82.**)
This subspecies is distinctive due to its even banding. In good examples the white, red and black rings are of roughly equal width and of clear colour. They tend to become suffused with black as the animal matures, but this is still one of the most attractive subspecies. A form in which the pale bands are inclined towards a pale pinkish-orange colour is sometimes known as the 'apricot' phase, but this is part of a natural range of variation rather than a distinct mutation. Although hardy, this is one of the more nervous subspecies, which resents too much handling.

Care and breeding are as for other milksnakes. This subspecies can be very prolific, producing up to three clutches of about seven eggs each season. The hatchlings are large and plump and normally accept newborn mice without trouble, although they sometimes live off their yolk reserves for several weeks after hatching and may refuse food at first. Once the young begin to feed they grow at a rapid rate.

New Mexican milksnake, *Lampropeltis triangulum celaenops*

Lampropeltis triangulum celaenops – New Mexican Milksnake
This is a difficult subspecies to describe since it is so variable, probably because it intergrades with adjacent forms, especially *L. t. annulata*. Animals from the centre of the range have wide white bands with narrow black borders. The red areas become narrower on the flanks and are intermediate in shape between rings and saddles.

Care is as for the other milksnakes. This species is not widely bred because the hatchlings are rather small and are not always easy to start on newborn mice. However, some strains produce bigger hatchlings than others and the form may become more readily available in time.

Lampropeltis triangulum hondurensis – Honduran Milksnake (**In colour on pages 54 and 83.**)
Honduran milksnakes are the largest of the commonly available subspecies and may reach a length of 1.5 m (5 ft). Typical examples are bright red with 13-26 triads of black and white, but the so-called 'tangerine' phase, in which the white is replaced by bright orange, has become very popular and commands a higher price. A light chevron on the snout, pointing backwards,

is distinctive. This subspecies always becomes darker with age and some adults are almost entirely suffused with black. It is important, therefore, to try to examine the parents of offspring which are offered for sale.

General care and breeding are as for other milksnakes. Honduran milksnakes are easily cared for, but due to their size they require larger cages than most other milksnakes. Although they rarely bite, adults are active and somewhat nervous in disposition, and are likely to launch themselves out of the cage whenever it is opened. Females lay about six very large eggs which hatch after about 65 days at 28°C (82°F), and the hatchlings measure about 40 cm (16 in) in length. They feed readily on young mice right from the start, and grow quickly.

Lampropeltis triangulum nelsoni – Nelson's Milksnake
Nelson's milksnake comes from western Mexico, adjacent to the range of the Sinaloan milksnake, which it closely resembles. There is often confusion over the two subspecies and it can be helpful to know where the stock originated. The main differences are in the number of triads on the body (although there is some overlap): 13-18 in *nelsoni* (average 16); 10-16 in *sinaloae* (average 13). The black bands also tend to become wider dorsally in *nelsoni*, whereas they are more or less parallel in *sinaloae*. The first black band is broken beneath the throat in *nelsoni*, and complete in *sinaloae*.

This is a slender subspecies, growing to 1 m (3 ft) or more, and with wide red bands. It can

North American Ratsnakes (1)

Baird's ratsnake, *Elaphe bairdi*

Juvenile Baird's ratsnake, *Elaphe bairdi*

A corn snake from the Miami region: note how its background colour differs from that of the Okeetee example

Corn snake, *Elaphe guttata*, one of the most popular snakes, and easily maintained and bred in captivity. This specimen is from the Okeetee region of South Carolina

be nervous in disposition, but usually thrives in captivity under similar conditions to other milksnakes. Clutch sizes tend to be slightly smaller than the others, about 6 eggs on average.

Lampropeltis triangulum sinaloae – Sinaloan Milksnake (**In colour on page 83.**)
This is one of the most attractive milksnakes and is often in short supply despite the fact that it is bred in reasonably large numbers. The ground colour should be bright red, with clean black and white triads. (See above for differences from *L. t. nelsoni*.) There is little tendency to darken with age, although it is unrealistic to expect adults to be quite as bright as hatchlings, as with all milksnakes.

Care and breeding are as for other milksnakes. Clutches average about seven eggs and second clutches may be produced, but only if the female has been well conditioned. Like its close relative, Nelson's milksnake, and the Honduran milksnake, this is not always one of the easiest subspecies to handle due to its rapid darting movements.

Lampropeltis triangulum syspila – Red Milksnake
This subspecies, from northern North America, has red saddles rather than circles. Each is elongated and bordered with black, and the areas between are yellow or cream. It grows to almost 1 m (3 ft) in total length.

Care and breeding are as for other milksnakes, although this form is more tolerant of cold and would almost certainly require a substantial period of cooling if it is to breed. There are few reports of captive-breeding, but the hatchlings measure about 20 cm (8 in) and may therefore present problems with feeding.

Other milksnakes
Many other subspecies of *Lampropeltis triangulum* are known from North, Central and South America. Many of these are infrequently available because they are rare, because they are not as attractive as the forms mentioned or, often, because the hatchlings are so tiny that feeding them creates a problem. However, specialists who are prepared to go to a little trouble may well find that some of these less-popular subspecies are very rewarding.

The striped form of the Californian kingsnake, which is only found in the area around San Diego

MUTATIONS

Mutations occur in nature through sudden and random changes in the genetic make-up of an animal. Most mutations result in the early death of the animal or in a failure to develop, but mutations such as those affecting coloration may become fixed in a population. Most of the colour variants which are found in captive-bred snakes have arisen by mutation, either in the wild or in the course of a captive-breeding programme. Further details of how these types may be proliferated are given under SELECTIVE BREEDING, while some of the more commonly seen colour mutations are described under the headings ALBINOS, AMELANISTIC, ANERYTHRISTIC and MELANISTIC SNAKES.

A number of snake species occur in more than one form. The best known example is probably that of the Californian kingsnake, *Lampropeltis getulus californiae*, of which this is the banded form

P

POLYMORPHISM

Polymorphism is a phenomenon in which more than one pattern or colour type exists within a single species or subspecies. It should not be confused with instances in which occasional mutants, such as albinos, occur by chance and have been developed into strains through captive-breeding programmes, nor with cases where juveniles are marked differently from adults of the same species. Several snakes are polymorphic: examples are the Californian kingsnake, which may be banded or striped, and the grey-banded kingsnake, which occurs in four distinct morphs or 'phases'. Polymorphic types are usually controlled by one or more genes, and these can often be manipulated to produce the types required in much the same manner as characteristics such as albinism, (see SELECTIVE BREEDING). (**In colour on pages 55, 115 and 119**.)

PYTHONS

The pythons are usually regarded as part of the same family as the boas, from which they differ by having heat-sensitive pits within the scales bordering the upper lip (boas have these pits *between* the scales) and in laying eggs. With one exception, all pythons occur in the Old World, with the greatest diversity of species in the Australasian region.

Many of these species grow very large and, when adult, they require similar accommodation to that described for the common boa, that is, a large walk-in type of cage possibly furnished with sturdy branches and/or a raised shelf on which the animal can lie under a heat source. Hygiene dictates that the layout of the cage be kept simple, with newspaper or wood shavings as a substrate. Food may consist of rabbits or larger mammals, and safety precautions should be taken during feeding (see HANDLING). Small pythons can be accommodated in much the same manner as colubrids.

Except for a few species, pythons can be successfully bred in captivity by following much the same regime as for other snakes: they are cooled off slightly during the winter and warmed up again in the spring. Some species mate during the cool season, and so the males and females must obviously be kept together during this period. Others mate when the temperature is raised. Females of some of the larger species often display strange behaviour when gravid: they may bask in bizarre positions, sometimes lying on their backs, in order to expose the developing eggs to heat. Females of the genus *Python*, and some others, coil around the clutch of eggs when they have been laid and remain with them until they hatch. This parental care is primarily protective – the large white eggs would be conspicuous and therefore vulnerable to predation in the wild. By covering the eggs, the female disguises them and can also repel possible predators. One or two species have taken their parental care a stage further by raising the temperature of the eggs through a physiological process not fully understood. Females of these species twitch repeatedly while they are coiled around the eggs and it has been shown that they are able to exert a fair degree of control over the incubation temperature. In addition, the tightness of the coils is adjusted according to the humidity.

In captivity, eggs of these species may be removed to an artificial incubator, and this usually gives a higher hatch-rate. This does not appear to have any adverse affect on the female, although she may be more aggressive than usual during the eggs' removal and for a few days afterwards. Natural egg-brooding, however, is an interesting spectacle and the decision may be made to leave the clutch with the female. If this is the case, all other snakes should be removed from the cage if this has not already been done, and the humidity of the cage should be increased by spraying: if the female covers the eggs completely with her body, this is an indication that they are becoming too dry. Eggs which are rejected by the female are usually infertile, but may be placed in an incubator if there is any doubt. The behaviour of the female should be carefully watched. If there is any sign that she has decided to desert the eggs before they are due to hatch, they should be removed. Brooding females will often refuse food, but occasionally leave the clutch at intervals in order to drink. Once the eggs begin to hatch the female will take no further interest and is best removed in case she accidentally crushes the young.

The 'true' pythons, genus *Python*, are dealt with first, followed by the Australasian species and the Mexican python.

GENUS *Python*

Python curtus – Blood Python (In colour on page 86.)

This South-East Asian species grows to about 2 m (6 ft) in total length but is extremely heavily built, with a short, sharply tapering tail. The markings are irregular and consist of connected chestnut-brown blotches on a cream or beige background, fading to white on the lower flanks. Some individuals, reportedly those from Sumatra, have an overall wash of red, from which the species gets its common name. The head is narrow, and the cheeks and upper lips are dark brown, almost black.

Imported blood pythons suffer from the same drawbacks as other South-East Asian snakes: heavy parasite burdens compounded with stress due to bad handling and poor housing. They are notoriously difficult to feed and can also be of uncertain temperament. By contrast, captive-bred individuals are amongst the most simple and pleasant snakes to keep: they feed well and grow rapidly, are not aggressive and breed regularly. They can be housed in almost any suitable container and maintained at a temperature of 25-30°C (77-86°F). Simple set-ups are best, with a substrate of newspaper or wood shavings, and a large water bowl is appreciated since their natural habitat tends to be humid. A hide-box is usually unnecessary (for captive-bred animals at least). They require a diet of mice or rats according to size.

Regular captive breeding has only taken place recently, due to the difficulty in keeping adults alive long enough for this to occur. It seems that they mature in three to four years. Breeding adults should be cooled slightly in the winter. The females lay clutches of about ten eggs, which are brooded under normal circumstances but are usually removed for artificial incubation under captive conditions. The eggs can be incubated at about 30°C (86°F), when they will hatch in 60-90 days. The young are plump, measure 30-45 cm (12-18 in) and usually begin feeding on mice soon after hatching.

Python molurus – Burmese Python, Indian Python (In colour on page 86.)

Two, or possibly three, subspecies of this large python are recognised. *P. m. molurus* is the Indian python, sometimes known as the light-phase Indian. *P. m. bivittatus* is the Burmese python or dark-phase Indian. *P. m. pimbura* is a dubious subspecies which is found in Sri Lanka. The Indian and Sri Lankan forms are beige with large, darker brown blotches. The head may be suffused with pink, more noticeable in juveniles than adults. The

Burmese python has a similar pattern but the colours are darker and much richer, with rich brown blotches on a yellowish background, fading to almost white on the flanks and underside.

The Burmese subspecies is the one most commonly seen, as the other two are protected. An albino form, in which the markings are of bright yellow on a white background, is now bred in fairly large numbers and will become more readily available in the future. Another mutation, known as the 'green' Burmese, affects the arrangement of the markings. These are reduced to a single narrow line running along the back, and the remainder of the snake is brown. With the eye of faith it is possible to discern an elusive green tinge to the snake, hence its popular name.

All these forms are large, up to 6 or even 7 m (20-23 ft) in the case of the Burmese, slightly smaller in the others. They can grow at an enormous rate, attaining sexual maturity at 3-4 m (10-13 ft), less than two years after hatching. This should be carefully considered when buying young specimens, because adults require enormous cages, a large quantity of food in the form of rabbits, chickens, etc., and can be difficult to handle due to their length and weight. They are normally fairly tractable, however, and are probably the best of the giant snakes to keep in captivity.

A temperature of 25-30°C (77-86°F) is required, with a distinct drop in the winter, which is their breeding season. Adults usually mate shortly after the temperature is lowered and the eggs, numbering up to 100 but usually closer to 30, are laid two to four months later, by which time the temperature should have been returned to normal. Females spend a great deal of time basking just prior to laying their eggs, and a heat lamp is useful at this time. The eggs are gathered into a conical heap by the female as they are laid and she subsequently coils around them. It has been shown that she has a limited ability to raise their temperature, a process which is associated with repeated twitching movements. Some females become aggressive at this time, so removing the eggs, if this is considered necessary, can be an interesting experience! At a temperature of 30°C (86°F), the eggs will hatch in about 60-70 days and the very attractive young invariably begin feeding on small mice as soon as they have completed their initial shed.

The predictable nature of their breeding habits and their large clutches make this a prolific species, and captive-bred young are freely available at the appropriate time of year, usually in the early summer.

The royal python, *Python regius*, is popular with beginners but is not always the best choice

Python regius – Royal Python, Ball Python

This is a short, stout python, similar in form to the blood python but smaller. This species rarely exceeds 1.2 m (4 ft) and is dark brown with light-edged tan blotches. These pythons are attractive and exceedingly good tempered and have therefore become popular pets. Unfortunately, they often refuse to feed with any degree of regularity, and this can cause concern. They seem naturally inclined to fast for long periods of time without losing weight, but every effort should be made to induce feeding on a regular basis if they are to thrive.

They are not particularly active and therefore require only a medium-sized cage, which should be heated to 25-30°C (77-86°F). A hide-box is appreciated, as is a large bowl of water in which they can soak. Other furnishings are superfluous. It may be necessary to try several different prey items in order to initiate feeding, and these may include mice, rats, gerbils and hamsters, all of which should be offered dead. Raising the humidity by copious spraying at feeding time sometimes has the desired effect, as does placing the snake in a small container with its food, but persistent failure to eat, accompanied by loss of weight (usually after

several months have elapsed) necessitates a visit to a vet, who may be able to stimulate the snake's appetite with a vitamin injection.

Breeding has not been achieved on a reliable basis, most of the hatchling snakes which appear on the market having originated from eggs which were already forming in the female when she was captured. These young pythons often do better than wild-caught adults and are probably the best hope of establishing a breeding colony. Small clutches of up to seven eggs are laid, and females normally brood their eggs, although this is not recommended for captive animals because females (especially if newly imported) generally make poor mothers when in captivity. The incubation can last from 40-80 days, depending on conditions, and the young measure about 40 cm (16 in).

Python reticulatus – Reticulated Python

This enormous python may grow to 9 m (30 ft) in length and has a wide range over much of South-East Asia. It can best be described as a species with an attractive pattern and an ugly disposition. The ground colour is yellow, largely obscured by a complex arrangement of black-and-white reticulations.

In captivity, it requires the usual large enclosure with a powerful heat source. It eats any large mammal, including people (there are several well-documented cases!), but can be maintained equally well on rats, rabbits and larger domestic animals. It will breed in captivity under the same conditions as the Burmese python, but it is difficult to understand why anybody would wish to do so.

Python sebae – African Rock Python

The largest of the African pythons, this species can grow to 5 or 6 m (16-20 ft). It is brown with darker markings on the back and flanks. It is not widely kept in captivity, but may be treated in the same manner as the Burmese python. This species is very tolerant of cold, and is generally undemanding, but is often untrustworthy and large individuals should be handled with caution. Clutches of 30-50 eggs are laid in early summer and are naturally brooded by the mother. They hatch after two to three months and the hatchlings measure 45-55 cm (18-22 in).

GROUP 2

AUSTRALIAN PYTHONS

The taxonomy of Australian pythons is chaotic at present and many of the following species are often listed under different generic names. They comprise four genera, as recognised here.

Aspidites, with two species endemic to Australia.
Chondropython, with a single species from New Guinea and extreme northern Queensland, Australia.
Liasis, with a number of species in New Guinea, Australia and Indonesia – many of these have been placed in separate genera over the years but no single arrangement has been generally accepted.
Morelia, with a single species having a wide range over much of Australia and New Guinea.

Only the most commonly available species are dealt with.

Aspidites melanocephalus – Black-headed Python

This is a rare Australian species, growing to about 2 m (6½ ft) with a brown and black barred body and jet black head and neck. They are kept in a similar manner to the Burmese python, and fed on rodents, although their natural diet includes a large proportion of other snakes. Black-headed pythons are usually kept only by wealthy specialists owing to the difficulties in obtaining specimens. However, they have been bred in captivity, where up to 12 eggs are laid. These hatch in two to three months and the young measure 65-70 cm (26-28 in).

Note: the other species of *Aspidites*, *A. ramsayi*, is known as the woma and is even less frequently seen.

Chondropython viridis – Green Tree Python

Definitely one of the most attractive snakes, this species grows to about 1.5 m (5 ft) and is bright green in colour with a series of white markings down its back. Like its South American relative, the emerald tree boa, this species drapes itself artistically over horizontal boughs, with its head resting in the centre of its coils. Juveniles are bright yellow or dull red, again paralleling the boa.

This arboreal python requires a tall cage with a natural or artificial horizontal perch, where it will spend the majority of its time. A temperature of 25-30°C (77-86°F) should be provided at all times, and humidity should be maintained at a fairly high level by regular spraying. Food, in the form of rodents or birds, is best offered on feeding forceps.

Breeding is stimulated by raising the temperature after a period of cooling off at about 20-25°C (68-77°F), with an accompanying increase in humidity, brought about by frequent spraying and reducing the area of ventilation. The snakes mate while clinging to their perch, and their tails remain intertwined for long periods of time while copulation takes place. Females will come down to the ground to lay their eggs in containers of moist material such as chopped sphagnum moss, but it may be preferable to fix this container (firmly!) high up in the cage. The eggs are brooded, but most successful attempts at breeding have occurred when they are removed to an artificial incubator. At 30°C (86°F) they hatch after about 50 days, and the young, measuring 25-30 cm (10-12 in) nearly always require force-feeding at first.

Liasis boa – Bismarck Ring Python

This strange species of python from the Bismarck Archipelago, is sometimes placed in a separate genus, *Bothrochilus*. It grows to about 1.5 m (5 ft), and the hatchlings are most spectacular, being encircled with black and orange bands for the length of their body. Unfortunately, these markings become dull and indistinct as the snakes grow. Ring pythons are rarely seen in captivity at present, but have been bred on a number of occasions. About ten eggs are laid and the females may brood these under natural conditions. General husbandry should be as for D'Albertis' python (below).

The green tree python, *Chondropython viridis*, bears a close resemblance to the emerald tree boa, *Corallus canina*

Liasis albertisi – D'Albertis' Python (In colour on page 91.)

Typical D'Albertis' pythons are iridescent bronze with a black head and white lips. They grow to about 2 m (6½ ft) in length and are relatively slender snakes. This species can be bad tempered but captive-raised animals are not too difficult to handle. They require medium-sized to large cages, with a temperature of 25-30°C (77-86°F), and benefit from a hide-box. They eat rodents readily and can be induced to breed once they have settled in a captive environment. They should be cooled down during the winter to about 20-22°C (68-72°F). They lay about 12 eggs which hatch after 60-70 days and the young measure about 30 cm (1 ft). These appear to feed more readily if kept in a humid environment.

Notes: *Liasis mackloti* is similar but lacks the bronze colour on the body and the black head,

being uniformly greyish, sometimes with irregular black spots, while Boelen's python, *Liasis boeleni*, is one of the most spectacular of all snakes, being velvety black with angled white bars on the flanks and white streaks on the upper jaw. Neither of these species is freely available and the latter is potentially one of the world's most valuable reptiles.

Liasis childreni – Children's Python (In colour on page 90.)

This is a small python, growing to 1 m (3 ft) or less. Children's pythons (named for a biologist, not due to their suitability as family pets!) are pale brown with irregular mottled darker brown markings on the back and flanks, sometimes arranged into vague crossbars. The underside is almost white. This is an easy python to keep and breed and is recommended in lieu of most of the above species for those who are attracted by the thought of owning a python. They may be treated in the same way as colubrid snakes: kept in small boxes or cages with a thermal gradient providing temperatures up to about 30°C (86°F), and a substrate of newspaper or wood shavings. They feed on mice of an appropriate size.

Breeding is induced by cooling them down to about 15°C (59°F) during the winter and clutches consist of about ten eggs. These may be brooded by the female or removed to an incubator, and will hatch after about 60 days. The hatchlings measure about 25 cm (10 in) and take newborn mice readily. They have large appetites, grow rapidly and have the potential to mature in less than two years, although three years is more common.

Notes: *Liasis stimsoni*, Stimson's python, is a dwarf version of Children's python and is sometimes known as a 'desert phase' Children's python. This species has been established recently, along with *Liasis perthensis*, both species being formerly included in *L. childreni*. Stimson's python is smaller, at about 80 cm (32 in), than Children's python, and rather paler in colour. Its care and breeding are exactly as for Children's python and the small hatchlings are equally prepared to accept newborn mice, despite their seemingly delicate appearance. (**In colour on page 90.**) *L. perthensis* is even smaller, with a maximum size of about 65 cm (26 in), but probably feeds on geckos: if so, this would preclude its suitability as a captive.

Morelia spilotes – Carpet Python, Diamond Python (In colour on page 91.)

This is a variable species with a wide range. The subspecies *Morelia spilotes spilotes* is known as the diamond python and grows to about 3 m (10 ft) in length. It is black or dark grey in colour, with clear white markings scattered over the entire body. Sometimes these coalesce in places to form larger white areas or 'diamonds'.

The more frequently seen subspecies is the carpet python, *Morelia spilotes variegata*. This, in turn, is variable, with several geographic races recognisable. It is typically dark grey, with paler blotches arranged along its back. These may be in two parallel rows, or connected to each other either across the back or longitudinally. The ground colour may also vary, being reddish, brown or yellow. Individuals from Queensland are dark grey with yellow or gold markings and are often known as 'jungle phase' or 'tiger' carpet pythons. The latter form is especially sought after and commands a higher price than the others (except the diamond python).

Care of these snakes, irrespective of their colour or name, is similar and quite straightforward. They are partially arboreal and benefit from a tall cage with a stout branch for climbing. They feed readily on rodents and require a temperature of 25-30°C (77-86°F), which should be reduced during the winter if it is hoped to breed from them. Females lay 15-20 eggs, although larger clutches, of up to 50 or more, are on record, and they will brood these if given the chance. Incubation takes about 60-65 days and the hatchlings are long (40-50 cm/16-20 in) but slender. They will normally feed without too much persuasion but sometimes require mice which are made to appear active (i.e. held in forceps and jiggled around in front of the snake) in order to stimulate a feeding response.

GROUP 3

NEW WORLD PYTHONS

Loxocemus bicolor – Mexican Burrowing Python (In colour on page 123.)

This species of python is found in Mexico and Honduras and is the only species of python found in the New World. Its relationships with other pythons are unclear, as it lives in a part of the world where pythons have no right to be! It is sometimes placed in its own family or grouped with the sunbeam snake, *Xenopeltis unicolor*. It grows to just over 1 m (3 ft) in length and is a uniform dark grey above and pale grey or cream beneath. Sometimes there are odd patches of white scales scattered irregularly over the back and flanks. Its scales are smooth and highly iridescent, and the head is wedge-shaped with a slightly upturned snout, in keeping with its burrowing habits.

This dwarf python is rarely seen in captivity, but appears to do very well in a small box or cage with a good depth of wood shavings or similar substrate into which it can burrow. A temperature of about 25-30°C (77-86°F) seems to suit it and it feeds readily enough on mice. Breeding information is not available.

Q

R

QUARANTINE

The largest threat to an established collection of snakes is the introduction of disease through newly acquired animals. If new specimens are only purchased from a reliable dealer or breeder, and are inspected carefully before purchase, this risk can be minimised, but it is still good policy to house new animals separately. Treat these animal as though they are diseased. Keep them on a sterile substrate, such as paper towelling, so that they can be thoroughly cleaned and faeces can be checked for parasites, etc. Handle them as little as possible and always *after* the established snakes have been serviced, and use a different set of tools and instruments (probes, scoops, etc.) for them, or sterilise such tools thoroughly after use. Never mix up water bowls, hide-boxes, etc. If at all possible, keep them in a separate room.

The period of time for which quarantine should be maintained is difficult to assess. Many snake diseases can be present for a long time before the snake becomes obviously sick, but careful observation of the animal's appearance, the way in which it sheds its skin, and whether it is eating and digesting its food properly should give a good indication of whether it is healthy (see HEALTH). If, after a month or two, everything seems to be functioning correctly, it is probably safe to house the new animal alongside the rest of the collection, but much depends on the owner's powers of observation and his or her sensitivity as to when everything is 'right' with the animal. Prophylactic treatment with drugs during quarantine is not normally recommended.

RACERS AND WHIPSNAKES

Two genera, *Coluber* and *Masticophis*, are so similar in their habits that they will be dealt with here together. In North America the *Coluber* species are known as racers, and the *Masticophis* species as whipsnakes or coachwhips. Confusingly, the European species of *Coluber* are known as whipsnakes. (There are no European *Masticophis* species.)

All are long, slender, diurnal snakes which are fast-moving and active hunters of lizards, snakes, small rodents and birds. All grow to at least 1 m (3 ft), and the coachwhip, *Masticophis flagellum*, can easily exceed 2 m (6½ ft) in length. Coloration varies from solid black, in the case of *Coluber constrictor* and certain populations of the European species *C. viridiflavus*, through browns and yellows, to brick-red in the case of the red racer of California. Several forms are patterned with longitudinal stripes.

Unfortunately, despite their attractive appearance, racers and whipsnakes do not often make satisfactory captives. They are so active that they require very large cages, otherwise they will constantly rub their noses raw. Furthermore, most of them bite savagely and only rarely tame down in captivity. They require a high temperature – up to 30°C (86°F) during the day – and like to bask beneath a spotlight. A diet of mice may be accepted by some, but others will refuse to eat anything other than lizards, while many refuse to feed altogether. They are not regularly bred in captivity.

RATSNAKES

The ratsnakes form a huge and widespread group of snakes, formerly all placed in the genus *Elaphe*, but currently undergoing some revision. For the sake of convenience, they will all be dealt with together here, with the species accounts divided into North American, European and Asian species.

Although there is some variation, most ratsnakes are medium-sized, with keeled scales, a slender but powerful body, and an elegant wedge-shaped head. Many species are attractively marked and the majority are ideal subjects for keeping and breeding, although some have become more popular than others.

They require fairly large cages as adults, since

they are quite active. A few species like to climb so they should be provided with a tall cage and a stout branch. Otherwise, their maintenance is straightforward: they are, with a few exceptions, rodent-eaters, and hatchlings are normally easily started on newborn mice. They require a thermal gradient, with an opportunity to reach a temperature of around 25°C (77°F) for at least part of the day. In winter, adults should be cooled down to about 12-15°C (54-59°F), although certain of the tropical species may require a consistently higher temperature than this. The commonly kept species all breed readily in captivity, provided they have been cooled off, although some are more prolific than others. Colour variations have arisen in several species and subspecies and many of these are perpetuated through the efforts of commercial and private breeders, so there is ample scope within this single group of snakes to build up a varied and interesting collection.

GROUP 1

NORTH AMERICAN SPECIES

The North American ratsnakes are by far the most popular and the easiest to obtain. Practically every species is bred in captivity, often in enormous numbers. These are temperate and sub-tropical snakes which require a temperature of around 25°C (77°F) for at least part of the day while they are active. All species can be cooled down during the winter, and this is essential for some species if they are to breed. A characteristic shared by several of the species is having a distinct juvenile pattern, which changes as the animals mature.

The Trans-Pecos ratsnake, *Elaphe subocularis*, is an attractive species with noticeably larger eyes than other ratsnakes

Elaphe bairdi – Baird's Ratsnake (In colour on page 94.)

Found in southern Texas and northern Mexico, juvenile Baird's ratsnakes are grey with about 40 dark bars across their back. As they grow, these fade gradually until the snake is grey overall, but with a suffusion of orange or salmon-pink coloration at the base of each scale. The heads and necks tend towards orange or rust, and four dusky lines may develop along the body. The scales are only weakly keeled and the snakes take on a satin-like lustre when in good condition. They rarely bite in captivity, even if wild-caught. Adults grow to slightly more than 1 m (3 ft). There is a naturally occurring form from northern Mexico, in which the body has more orange pigmentation and the head is solid grey.

Care and breeding are as in the genus description. Baird's ratsnakes have only become well known in recent years and are not as widely bred as several other North American ratsnakes. They lay up to 14 eggs, averaging around nine per clutch, and these hatch in about 65 days if incubated at 28°C (82°F). The hatchlings measure 35-40 cm (14-16 in) and begin to feed on newborn mice without problems.

Elaphe guttata – Corn Snake or Red Ratsnake, Plains Ratsnake

Two subspecies are widely recognised.

Elaphe guttata guttata – Corn Snake, Red Ratsnake (In colour on page 95.

This subspecies grows to about 1 m (3 ft) in length and is one of the most beautiful ratsnakes. Well-marked corn snakes are pale orange or straw-coloured, with a series of large bright red saddles along the back. Each saddle is edged in black, and the head is marked with two chevrons of red. The underside consists of white and black squares, arranged into a chequered pattern. The best examples of this type are usually known as Okeetee corn snakes, and come from a population renowned for its bright colours. In some other populations the ground colour can be grey or silver and the blotches may be orange or wine-red, while in the southern parts of Florida there is a form in which the black borders to the saddles are reduced or absent (sometimes known as the rosy ratsnake, *E. guttata rosacea*). Captive-bred corn snakes are often intermediate in colour and markings, but all are attractive.

In addition to this natural variation in colour and markings, a whole host of colour mutations have appeared in this species, and these are all bred successfully in captivity and are therefore widely available. These comprise the following strains:

Amelanistic (red albino) in which the black is missing altogether and the snakes have red or pink markings on an almost clear white background. The eyes are pink. (**In colour on page 119.**)

Anerythristic (black albino), which is the reverse of the above, i.e. all the red pigment is missing and the snakes show only the black edgings to the saddles, which are grey. (**In colour on page 119**.)

Albino (snow corns) where both the above mutations have been combined to produce snakes with no red or black pigment. They are plain white with only faint traces of markings. (**In colour on page 122**.)

European ratsnakes, such as the four-lined snake, *Elaphe quatuorlineata*, are not as popular among snake-keepers as the North American species, although they usually adapt to captivity just as well

Blood-red, in which the adults are solid red in colour and lose almost all trace of the dorsal blotches.

Striped, in which the red saddles are replaced by a continuous broad red stripe along the back.

With the exception of one or two of the rather inbred mutant strains, corn snakes are among the simplest snakes to keep and breed. Some strains tend to produce small hatchlings which are reluctant to start feeding on newborn mice, but, generally speaking, they feed and grow at a rapid rate, and may be large enough to breed within a year (although sexual maturity within two years is a more realistic goal). Females mate in the spring and lay clutches of 12 or more eggs about one month later. These hatch in about 60 days if kept at 28°C (82°F). It is easily possible to obtain a second clutch of eggs later in the year. Selective breeding of any of the colour variants listed above requires some knowledge of elementary genetics and an appreciation of the dangers of inbreeding depression. See under SELECTIVE BREEDING and INBREEDING.

Elaphe guttata emoryi – Plains Ratsnake
The plains ratsnake is found further west than the corn snake and is overlooked somewhat because its colours cannot compare with those of that species. Nevertheless, it is attractively marked with a series of well-defined brown or olive blotches on a pale grey background (rather similar to the 'black albino' form of the corn

snake in fact). It also tends to be rather more robust than the corn snake and the hatchlings are larger. In all other respects, including its care in captivity, it is similar to the corn snake.

Elaphe obsoleta – **Common Ratsnake**

The most widespread of the American ratsnakes, this species occurs in a variety of distinct subspecies, all of which are suitable for captivity. All require large cages since they can grow to almost 2 m (6½ ft) in length and are active snakes. They all like to climb occasionally, although this is not an essential activity. Large specimens will eat adult rats, but mice are a more appropriate food for the majority.

Breeding is easily achieved. After a cooling-off period, adults mate in the spring and the females lay up to 40 eggs (typically 12-20), about five weeks later. They may lay two clutches during the season if well conditioned. The eggs hatch in 65-70 days at an incubation temperature of 28°C (82°F) and the hatchlings measure 30-45cm (12-18 in), and are vigorous and good feeders. Rearing them presents few problems and they can reach breeding size in two years. The subspecies are:

Elaphe obsoleta lindheimeri – Texas Ratsnake
A variable blotched ratsnake from the Texas-Louisiana region, which is probably the least attractive and most aggressive form! Large adults can be formidable opponents.

Care should be as in the species account. Apart from the leucistic form (see below), which is not widely available yet, this is the least popular of the subspecies.

Variation: a leucistic mutation is available, in which all traces of colour are absent from the body and tail, but the eyes are dark grey.

Elaphe obsoleta obsoleta – Black Ratsnake
The black ratsnake comes from north-eastern North America, including some parts of Canada. Hatchlings are pale grey, with a series of distinct black or dark grey blotches along the back. As they grow, the ground colour becomes progressively darker until the snake is totally black, except for the chin, which is white. This subspecies intergrades with neighbouring forms, and the darkest and most attractive animals originate in the north of the range.

Care and breeding should be as in the species account.

Variation: an amelanistic strain is available, the animals being white or pale pink with darker pink blotches. (**In colour on page 18.**)

Elaphe obsoleta quadrivittata – Yellow Ratsnake (**In colour on page 114.**)
Found in Florida and up the south-eastern seaboard of North America, hatchlings of this subspecies start with much the same coloration as those of the black ratsnake, but the blotches gradually fade as the ground colour becomes yellow, and four indistinct longitudinal stripes appear along the body. Good examples are of a rich bright colour.

Care and breeding are as in the species account.

Elaphe obsoleta spiloides – Grey Ratsnake
This is the only subspecies in which the blotched markings of the hatchlings are retained in the adult. Well-marked examples from the centre of the range (the Gulf states) are pale silvery-grey in colour, with darker grey blotches.

Care and breeding are as in the species account.

Elaphe obsoleta rossalleni – Everglades Ratsnake
Possibly only a local variation of the yellow ratsnake, the Everglades form is, nevertheless, distinct enough to be worthy of attention. The very best examples, which are few and far between, are bright orange in colour with the usual four dusky lines down the body.

Care and breeding are as in the species account.

Bogertophis (= *Elaphe*) *rosaliae* – **Rosalia Ratsnake (In colour on page 114.)**

This is a plain-coloured reddish-brown ratsnake. Juveniles are paler than adults and have indistinct blotches, but these disappear with age. The head is narrow and the eyes are prominent.

This rare ratsnake is not frequently seen in captivity. Its natural habitat is the dry rocky gorges of Baja California, where relatively few specimens have been found, but its requirements in captivity are probably similar to those of other ratsnakes. It appears to be somewhat more delicate, however, but this could be due to the fact that most examples in captivity are wild-caught and therefore not as well adapted as captive-bred animals.

Bogertophis (= *Elaphe*) *subocularis* – **Trans-Pecos Ratsnake (In colour on page 115.)**

This is a most unusual ratsnake from the Big Bend and Trans-Pecos regions of Texas, and northern Mexico. The ground colour is pale yellow, ochre or tan, and the markings consist of black H-shaped crossbars. The head is unmarked and the huge eyes are among the most distinctive features. This species is very slender, and may reach 1.5 m (5 ft) or more in total length. It is nocturnal in habit.

Care and breeding are rather different from that of other ratsnakes. This species is a late breeder which mates as late as July. The eggs are laid four to six weeks later and hatch after about 70 days at 28°C (82°F), often well into the autumn or even winter. Clutches are small, rarely as many as eight, and more usually around four. The laying of a second clutch is possible but unusual. Hatchlings are very slender and their large eyes are even more startling. They usually begin to feed on newborn mice and should present few rearing difficulties.

Variation: a naturally occurring colour variant is the 'blond' phase, in which the markings are small and faded, giving a pale ghostly effect. (**In colour on page 115.**)

Senticolis (=*Elaphe*) *triaspis* – Green Ratsnake

Despite its common name, this slender ratsnake, which hails from North and Central America, and just enters the United States in southern Arizona, is usually brown or olive, although specimens from the northern part of its range (subspecies *intermedia*) often have a greenish tinge. Central American examples (e.g. subspecies *mutabilis*) are less attractive but more frequently available. Juveniles are blotched, and have a dark band across the head, joining the eyes.

Care and breeding are apparently as in the genus account, although this species is still something of a novelty and breeding records are few.

Elaphe vulpina – Fox Snake

This is a thick-set snake with rich brown blotches on a yellowish-brown background. Two subspecies, *E. v. vulpina* and *E. v. gloydi*, both occur in the cool northern regions of North America, including parts of Canada. These differ mainly in the number of blotches on the body, there being fewer, about 34, in *gloydi*.

Care and breeding are similar to other ratsnakes, but this species seems to require a long period of hibernation, no doubt due to its northern origins. It is not widely kept or bred, but is thought to produce clutches of six to ten eggs.

ASIAN RATSNAKES

Note that although all the species described here are at present included in the genus *Elaphe*, it seems certain than future revisions will indicate that at least some of them will be removed from this genus and renamed. At the moment, then, more than 20 species of ratsnakes are found throughout Asia and many of these are attractive and worthy of a place in the snake collection. Unfortunately, they are invariably imported under poor conditions and only a small proportion survive for any length of time: even healthy looking individuals may carry heavy parasite and bacterial loads and frequently die within a few weeks of purchase. Breeding stocks of a small number of species have been established by gathering the eggs from imported gravid females, which usually die shortly after laying, or by rigorous medication and patient conditioning of the odd wild-caught individual. Captive-bred hatchlings of the following species are now becoming more readily available, or will be in the future, and should be chosen wherever possible.

Elaphe bimaculata – Chinese Ratsnake, Chinese Leopard Snake (In colour on page 118.)

This species grows to about 80 cm (32 in) in length and is yellowish-grey or tan in colour, spotted or striped with darker brown or reddish-brown. The head is small and there is no distinct neck region.

Its care in captivity is similar to that of the North American ratsnakes but it may be maintained at a temperature of about 25°C (77°F) all year round. Due to their small heads, they require a diet of small mice, even when adult. Small clutches of about three or four elongated eggs are laid, and these hatch after a short incubation period of 30-40 days. The hatchlings are relatively large compared to the adults, and will usually take newborn mice, although some require force-feeding at first.

Elaphe helena – Indian Trinket Snake

This species grows to about 1.5 m (5 ft) and is of slender build. Adults and juveniles are similar in appearance and are greyish-brown to olive-brown in colour with darker markings. The front part of the body is crossed by irregular bars which usually have small white patches within them, but on the lower part of the body and tail the bars coalesce to form a continuous line along each flank. When annoyed, this species flattens its neck from side to side and spreads the skin, showing white flecks of interstitial skin.

Captive-bred trinket snakes are easily kept in captivity and require similar conditions to North American ratsnakes. They feed readily on mice and require a temperature of 25-30°C (77-86°F). A cooling-off period is recommended if they are to breed. Small clutches of up to ten eggs are laid and these hatch after a short incubation period. The hatchlings will readily accept newborn mice.

Elaphe mandarina – Mandarin Ratsnake (In colour on page 118.)

Certainly the most colourful of the Asian ratsnakes, *Elaphe mandarina* is totally different in appearance to any of the other members of the genus. It grows to about 1 m (3 ft), but is usually slightly less, and its grey body is marked with a single row of bright yellow blotches running right down the dorsal surface. Each blotch is surrounded with a wide black border, which widens dorsally and may touch the neighbouring black areas. The head is strikingly marked with black and yellow chevrons. It comes from southern China, where it is found at moderately high altitudes.

Thousands of wild-caught specimens must have been collected over the years but these have invariably died despite all the efforts of dedicated snake-keepers. It appears that they are heavily parasitised and suffer greatly from the stress of being transported and confined. However, eggs which are laid by wild specimens before they succumb have, on occasion, been successfully incubated, and once these reach sexual maturity it seems likely that a small trickle of captive-bred hatchlings will be available at some stage in the future. They require slightly cooler conditions than other ratsnakes – a temperature of 20-25°C (68-77°F) appears to be satisfactory – and rather more humidity. A substrate such as bark chippings would therefore seem to be appropriate, and this should be very lightly sprayed from time to time. A hiding place is essential since even captive-hatched animals are inclined to be nervous. They feed on mice of the appropriate size, and rearing the young does not appear to present any problems. Although captive-breeding has only rarely been achieved, a period of cooling during the winter, to about 12°C (54°F), appears to be necessary. Clutches range from three to ten eggs. These hatch after an incubation period of 50-55 days at a temperature of about 26°C (79°F), and rearing the young presents few problems.

Elaphe rufodorsata – Chinese Ratsnake

This is one of the smaller ratsnakes, reaching a maximum size of about 80 cm (32 in). Males tend to be somewhat smaller than females. The markings consist of four parallel lines running down the body, with those on the back being irregular in shape and sometimes broken into a series of loosely connecting lozenges. The colour is variable, but is often brown or tan with darker brown or olive markings.

This is a rather atypical ratsnake because it naturally favours a damp habitat and feeds largely on amphibians and fish. In captivity, however, it should be kept on a dry substrate, but given a large water bowl in which to soak. A summer temperature of 25-30°C (77-86°F) is required, and adults can usually be persuaded to accept young mice. A winter temperature of about 15°C (59°F) is needed if they are to breed, with mating taking place as soon as they are warmed up in the spring. This species gives birth to living young. Up to 15 are born after a gestation period of about 100 days, and these measure 15-20 cm (6-8 in). They should be kept in a fairly humid environment to begin with, and usually accept small fish readily. They can often be induced to take newborn mice as soon as they have doubled in size.

Elaphe schrenki – Russian Ratsnake

This is a medium-sized species, which grows to about 1.5 m (5 ft) in length. Coloration is variable, but is typically black or dark brown with narrow bands of white or yellow. Some individuals are more brightly marked than others. Russian ratsnakes (which are also found in parts of northern China), are easily kept in captivity, and require similar conditions to the North American species of *Elaphe*. A temperature of between 22 and 27°C (72-81°F) is suitable during the summer, but this species is very tolerant of cold and adults should be given a long cooling off period in the winter if it is hoped to breed from them.

Clutches of ten or more eggs are laid in the summer and these have a short incubation period – about 40 days at 28°C (82°F). The hatchlings measure about 30 cm (1 ft) in length, and although some may start to feed on newborn mice voluntarily, others will need to be force-fed for the first few meals.

Elaphe taeniura – Asiatic Ratsnake
(In colour on page 118.)

Elaphe taeniura is the largest Asian member of the genus, and possibly the largest *Elaphe* in the world, easily reaching 2-2.5 m (6½-8 ft) in length. It has a slender body and narrow graceful head with large eyes. There are a variety of forms, including at least six subspecies, of which *E. t. friesei* is the one most likely to be available, at least as captive-bred young. The various subspecies may be olive-green, brown or copper-coloured but the markings are complex. The most distinctive feature is a heavy black line running through the eye. The top of the head and neck is plain, but the front part of the body is marked with narrow crossbars of black. Further down, these are joined on the flanks by equally narrow longitudinal lines which gradually widen until they cover the greater part of the flanks. At this point, i.e. on the lower body and tail, the crossbars peter out and the pattern is one of a central yellow, brown or bronze stripe, bordered by distinct dark lines on the flanks. *E. t. ridleyi*, from Malaysia and Sumatra, is of interest because it inhabits caves and feeds largely on bats. It is very pale grey, almost white, in colour, with the markings arranged more strongly into stripes than in *E. t. friesei*, for instance. In all subspecies the tongue is dark blue with pale blue edges.

Breeding is fairly straightforward: after a short cooling-off period at about 15°C (59°F), the animals will mate and the female lays five to ten eggs about one month later. These hatch after about 60 days at 28°C (82°F) and the hatchlings measure 35-40 cm (14-16 in). They feed readily on newborn mice.

EUROPEAN RATSNAKES

European ratsnakes, of which there are four species, have attracted rather less attention than their North American relatives, and their care and breeding are not so well documented. However, all are rodent-eaters which breed in the spring and their general requirements are similar to those given in the genus account.

Elaphe longissima – Aesculapian Snake

This is a graceful and slender ratsnake, from central and eastern Europe, which is uniform olive-green or brown when adult, but blotched as a juvenile. There are usually scattered white flecks along the flanks.

It is not often kept in captivity, although it does reasonably well under the same conditions as other ratsnakes. Between six and twelve eggs are laid, which hatch in under 60 days at 28°C (82°F), and the hatchlings will usually accept newborn mice.

Elaphe quatuorlineata – Four-lined Snake

This is a large, heavy-bodied snake, a number of subspecies of which are recognised. All are found in various parts of south-eastern Europe and all begin life heavily marked with black blotches on a pale grey background. In the typical form, the blotches fade, to be replaced by four longitudinal stripes, whereas in other subspecies (e.g. *sauromates*) traces of the juvenile markings are retained throughout life.

Care and breeding are as for other ratsnakes, although four-lined snakes seem prone to a mysterious loss of appetite from time to time. Breeding has not been achieved too often, and captive-bred juveniles are rarely available.

Elaphe scalaris – Ladder Snake

Ladder snakes are found in south-western Europe, including some of the Mediterranean islands. They are medium-sized snakes, growing to around 1.5 m (5 ft) and adults are brown with four dark lines running along their bodies. The hatchlings are cream in colour, with dark crossbars joining the lines across the back, like a ladder.

Ladder snakes usually feed well in captivity, although they can be aggressive. Juveniles take newborn mice, but they are not widely kept or bred.

Elaphe situla – Leopard Snake

This is one of the smallest ratsnakes, rarely growing to more than 75 cm (30 in). It is also one of the prettiest. Leopard snakes are found in Italy, Greece, Yugoslavia and neighbouring parts of south-eastern Europe. They are highly variable in colour and markings. Typical examples are cream or pale yellow with a series of bright red blotches down the back. Sometimes these blotches are constricted in the middle, like dumb-bells, across the midline, or they may be completely divided into two parallel rows of smaller spots. In extreme cases, the markings consist of two parallel solid lines along the back. Snakes from certain parts of the range have brown blotches and are not nearly so attractive.

Leopard snakes either do very well in captivity or very badly, refusing all efforts to induce them to feed. Until the reasons for this are fully understood, there is little chance that they will be bred with any degree of regularity. They lay small clutches of about four eggs and the hatchlings are relatively large, measuring about 30 cm (1 ft) and capable of taking newborn mice.

RECORD-KEEPING

Some form of record-keeping is practically essential if any serious attempts are to be made to keep or breed snakes over a period of time. This can vary from the most detailed reports on the snakes' day-to-day activities, to very sparse and abbreviated notes.

The most commonly used form of record-keeping is to make out an index card for each individual. The heading gives information such as the species/subspecies and the colour variety if appropriate, the sex, date of hatching or acquisition, and the parents or supplier. It may be necessary to provide some means of identification in order to distinguish each snake from others of the same species – most snakes can be recognised by some unique marking such as a broken band, or a distinctively shaped marking on the head, and a rough sketch at the top of the card will serve as a reminder.

Subsequent records should include dates of feeding and shedding and any abnormal behaviour. It is a good idea to weigh each snake from time to time, especially females which are used for breeding, since body-weight is often a good indication of health, and these records should also be added to the card. Breeding records are often best kept apart from day-to-day records, for instance on the back of the card or in a separate file. They should comprise the date the snakes were put together, dates of any mating activity seen, the pre-laying shed, date of egg-laying and size of clutch, date of hatching, and number and sex of young hatched successfully. Over a period of time these records will provide a useful data-bank which can be used to predict the productivity of the colony, assess the suitability of techniques used (by comparing with other records), and may provide interesting material for an article in one of the herpetological society publications.

As an alternative to the index card system, electronic filing can be used if a personal computer is available. Although several good card index programmes are commercially available, it should not be too difficult to design one specifically for snake records, using a database system in which it is possible to calculate averages and so on.

RED-TAILED RACER, RED-TAILED RATSNAKE

This beautiful South-East Asian snake was formerly included in the genus *Elaphe* but is now classified as *Gonyosoma oxycephala*. It grows to about 2 m (6½ ft) in length and, apart from black-edged scales on the forepart of the body, is completely green except for the last portion of its tail, which is red or brown. The head is narrow and a dark line passes through the eye, which is also green. The tongue is bright blue. It is an arboreal snake and therefore of slender build.

Care of this species is quite straightforward provided that captive-bred or well-established wild-caught individuals are available. Most of the wild snakes imported carry a huge parasite burden as well as a selection of diseases, and these problems are exacerbated by the stress involved in their none-too-sympathetic handling and shipping. Most die shortly after arrival. Captive-bred animals are available in small numbers, and these should be purchased in preference to wild, imported stock.

Assuming that healthy animals are available, they require medium-sized cages. If a branch is provided, they will use this, although it is not strictly essential. It is sometimes thought that they require rather higher humidity than other colubrids, but this is probably not the case, at least with captive-bred young. A temperature of about 25-30°C (77-86°F) should be provided at all times, although small reductions at night and during the winter will not hurt. Adults will eat rodents readily, but young animals may need assistance, such as placing a small mouse in their mouth, after which they usually go on to swallow it.

Established pairs of red-tailed racers breed throughout the year, although the females may retain sperm, making the precise determination of a breeding season difficult. Clutches consist of five to eight eggs and their incubation period is prone to great variation, from 80-180 days having been recorded. Newly hatched young rarely accept mice straightaway but are quite easily force-fed (see FEEDING HATCHLINGS).

RINGNECK SNAKE

The ringneck snake, *Diadophis punctatus*, is a small, secretive species from North America. Although a number of subspecies are recognised (sometimes regarded as full species), in practice, the only form likely to be of interest to snake-keepers is the southern ringneck, *D. p. punctatus*, because the others are uncommon and may have difficult feeding preferences.

D. p. punctatus grows to about 30 cm (1 ft) and is brown, dark grey or black above and bright orange or red underneath. The characteristic which gives it its name is a prominent orange ring just behind the head. When alarmed, ringneck snakes raise the tail and coil it, corkscrew fashion, to expose the bright coloration – captives soon become tame and rarely display in this manner.

They are easily kept in a small cage or plastic box, which should have a substrate of pea-gravel or clay beads. One area should be covered with a shallow layer of leaf-litter or moist sphagnum moss and one or two pieces of flat bark or slate should be laid on top of this. Alternatively, a hide-box can be filled with damp leaves or moss. The cage should be lightly sprayed from time to time to maintain a humid, but not too damp, environment. Ringneck snakes will eat small amphibians, especially newts, and other snakes, but a diet of earthworms appears to be perfectly satisfactory in captivity. They lay eggs, but are not regularly bred in captivity.

SAND SNAKES (In colour on page 122.)

Superficially, the sand snakes resemble shovel-nosed snakes (q.v.) very closely, but they have 13 rather than 15 scale rows at mid-body and an inset lower jaw. They are even more highly adapted to the desert and live in fine, wind-blown sand, moving through it by 'sand-swimming'. Two species are currently recognised, and they are dealt with together since their requirements are probably similar.

Chilomeniscus cinctus, the banded sand snake, is cream in colour with a series of black or dark brown cross-bars, some of which may encircle the body, or be restricted to the dorsal surface. Animals from some localities have red pigment between the body bands, restricted to the upper dorsum. Its range includes much of Baja California, part of southern Arizona and adjacent parts of Sonora.

Chilomeniscus stramineus, the bandless sand snake, is restricted to the Cape Region of Baja California del Sur, and to parts of the Mexican mainland opposite this area, i.e. Sinaloa. In this species, the colour is a uniform brown, yellow or cinnamon, with a single, small black dot on each scale.

Their care in captivity is exactly as for the shovel-nosed snakes (see entry). They do not appear to have been bred successfully.

SELECTIVE BREEDING

Selective breeding involves mating certain individuals which show desirable characteristics, e.g. colour, pattern, etc., in order to retain or enhance these characteristics. It can be carried out quite simply just by mating together any two attractive snakes, keeping the most attractive of the resulting offspring and mating these to each other or back to one of the parents and so on. Over a period of time, the characteristic will become 'fixed' in the colony. However, this type of arbitrary selective breeding can easily lead to an inbreeding depression (see INBREEDING), and care must be taken to avoid this.

Other characteristics are not so simply retained in a colony and these characteristics are controlled by the laws of inheritance, sometimes known as Mendelian inheritance, in which certain genes are dominant over others. Therefore, a basic understanding of genetics is necessary to plan a breeding programme. Although the subject can be extensive and

North American Ratsnakes (2)

Juvenile yellow ratsnake, *Elaphe obsoleta quadrivittata*. The blotched pattern will give way to a striped one as the snake matures

The rosalia ratsnake, *Elaphe rosaliae*, has a limited range in Baja California, and has rarely been bred in captivity so far

Trans-Pecos ratsnake, *Elaphe subocularis*, typical form

Trans-Pecos ratsnake, *Elaphe subocularis*, the unusual blond phase

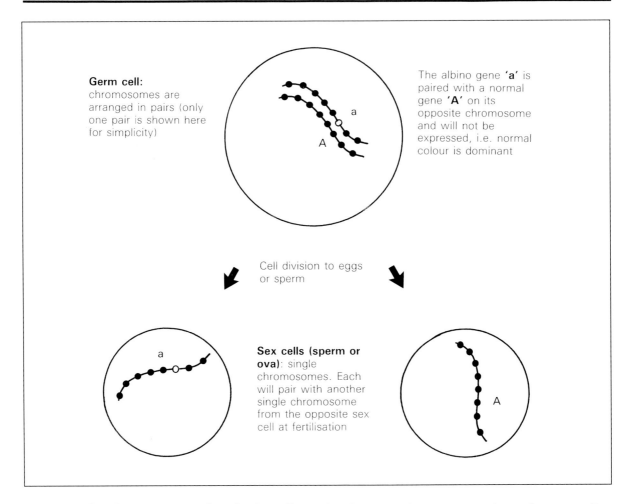

Germ cell:
chromosomes are
arranged in pairs (only
one pair is shown here
for simplicity)

The albino gene 'a' is
paired with a normal
gene 'A' on its
opposite chromosome
and will not be
expressed, i.e. normal
colour is dominant

Cell division to eggs
or sperm

Sex cells (sperm or
ova): single
chromosomes. Each
will pair with another
single chromosome
from the opposite sex
cell at fertilisation

complex, for the purposes of snake-breeding only the very simplest explanation is necessary.

Genes consist of small pieces of DNA which programme the cell to act in a certain way, for instance, to produce a certain pigment. The genes are arranged on chromosomes, each chromosome containing millions of genes. In the living cells, these chromosomes, and therefore the genes on them, are arranged in pairs, so there are two copies of each gene (there are exceptions to this but they do not concern us here). When the animal produces reproductive cells, however, the pairs split up so that each sperm or unfertilised egg contains only one copy of each chromosome (and therefore one copy of each gene). When the sperm and the egg come together in fertilisation, the copy from one parent combines with the copy from the other so that the paired arrangement is restored in the new individual.

Each pair of genes can comprise two similar genes, in which case it is said to be homozygous, or two different genes, in which case it is said to be heterozygous. Heterozygous pairs of genes often consist of one dominant gene (which is expressed) and one recessive gene (which is suppressed). In this way the characteristic concerned will depend on which genes are

Cell division in the testes or ovaries produces sex cells (gametes) which contain only one copy of each chromosome. In animals which are heterozygous for a colour mutation for instance, each sex cell has a 50:50 chance of containing the mutant gene

present and which is dominant. Thus a gene for albinism will normally be recessive to its opposite number, i.e. a gene for normal pigment, and so an animal containing a heterozygous, or mixed, pair will have normal coloration, even though it still 'carries' the albino gene and may pass it on to some of its offspring. However, if the gene for normal coloration is not present, i.e both genes programme for albinism (are homozygous for albinism), then the animal will be an albino.

In nature, recessive genes, such as those for albinism stay together only rarely because the character is disadvantageous and the resulting offspring will rarely survive for very long. In captivity, however, once an albino (or an animal which carries an albino gene) has been obtained, matings can be carried out in such a way that the genes are manipulated to produce the desired type of offspring.

This is best illustrated by a few examples. We

will use the albino mutation in these examples because it is well known, but the basic rules apply to any kind of recessive gene.

Example 1: starting with a single albino snake

Assuming the gene for albinism to be recessive, the albino snake must therefore have a pair of genes for albinism (otherwise it would not be an albino). By convention, the symbol for a recessive gene is lower case, e.g. 'a' for albino, and its normal counterpart is represented by the corresponding capital letter, e.g. 'A' for non-albino. A snake with two genes for albinism therefore has a pair of 'a' genes, 'aa' (it is homozygous for albinism). However, a snake with wild-type coloration may have either of two combinations of genes, AA (homozygous for wild-type), or Aa (heterozygous for albinism), with the effects of the A gene dominating those of the a gene. Let us assume, to start with, that the wild-type individual has a pair of non-albino genes, 'AA'.

Now, because an animal's sperm or eggs contain only one of the genes, and this is paired with the equivalent gene from its opposite number, i.e. the sperm or the egg of its mate, homozygous animals can only produce one type of gene, 'a' in the case of the albino and 'A' in the case of the wild type. Therefore all the offspring from this mating will be heterozygous, 'Aa' and look normal (see example 1).

Example 1 *(albino X normal)*

Parents   aa   X   AA

Types of sex cell
produced: a   A

Possible combinations
in offspring: Aa

(all heterozygous)

But what if the wild-type individual was actually heterozygous ('Aa')? In this case the chances are that about half of its sperm (let us say it is a male) will contain the 'a' gene and each of these, in combination with one of the 'a' genes from the albino female, will produce albinos in the brood. The other half will contain the 'A' gene and produce heterozygous offspring which will look wild-type in appearance (see example 1a). (Statistically, the proportions of wild-type to albino offspring in this situation is 50:50, but this is ruled by pure chance and the proportions can differ widely from one brood to another.) This, of course, is one way of finding out if a wild-type individual is carrying an albino gene or not (known as progeny-testing).

Example 1a *(albino X heterozygous)*

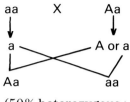

(50% heterozygous :
50% albino)

Example 2: mating two heterozygous animals

The same basic rule applies to mating two heterozygous animals, but here both kinds of wild-type snake may be produced as well as a number of albinos (see example). The important point here is that roughly three-quarters of the brood will have wild-type coloration but there is no way of telling which are heterozygous and which are homozygous for the wild-type without doing another series of test crosses, as outlined in example 1. This is therefore not an efficient way of selective breeding. Whenever possible, matings should be carried out between animals of known genetic make-up so that the results can be predicted (see example 2).

Example 2 *(heterozygous X heterozygous)*

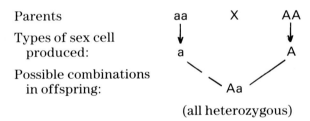

(50% heterozygous : 25% normal : 25% albino)

(75% *look* normal)

Example 3: outbreeding in order to introduce fresh blood (see INBREEDING)

In order to avoid inbreeding depression in a strain of snakes, it is frequently necessary to find an unrelated individual with which to mate some animals. Assuming that this is a wild-caught individual, and that it is mated to a pure albino, all offspring produced from such a mating will be heterozygous (as in example 1). As we have seen in example 2, it is not good practice to mate two heterozygous animals together, so the best course is to mate some of the offspring back to their albino parent (i.e. a 'back-cross'). Roughly half of the next generation will then be albino, and the other half will be heterozygous (as in example 2), but both types will also contain other genes from the wild individual and this will increase their vigour and reduce the chances of inbreeding depression occurring (see example 3).

Asian Ratsnakes

Mandarin ratsnake, *Elaphe mandarina*, an unusual and attractive ratsnake from China

Asian ratsnake, *Elaphe taeniura friesei*

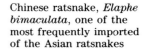

Chinese ratsnake, *Elaphe bimaculata*, one of the most frequently imported of the Asian ratsnakes

Cornsnake Mutations

The amelanistic form of the corn snake, *Elaphe guttata*, in which the black pigment is lacking

The anerythristic form of the corn snake, *Elaphe guttata*, in which the red pigment is lacking

Snow corn, *Elaphe guttata*, in which both red and black pigments are missing

Example 3 *(back cross)*

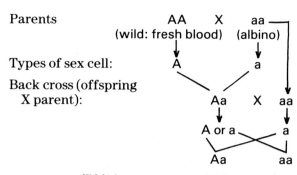

Parents   AA   X   aa
(wild: fresh blood) (albino)

Types of sex cell: A   a

Back cross (offspring
    X parent):   Aa   X   aa

                    A or a   a
                      Aa   aa

(50% heterozygous : 50% albino)

(both types contain some fresh blood)

So far we have been discussing fairly simple mechanisms, but certain colour variants consist of a combination of two or more mutant genes. For instance, in the case of corn snakes, there is a mutation which prevents only the black pigment from being produced giving rise to 'amelanistic' animals (i.e. no black markings), and another which prevents only the red pigment from being formed, giving rise to 'anerythristic' animals (i.e. no red markings, the so-called 'black albino' corn snakes). Both these forms are controlled exactly as described above. What happens when an amelanistic animal is mated with an anerythristic animal? Since the genes for amelanism and anerythrism behave independently of one another, all the offspring will be heterozygous for both characteristics and therefore they will all have wild-type markings! (They are usually known as double heterozygous.) Now, by crossing two of these double heterozygous snakes it is possible to produce a small number of offspring which can produce neither black nor red pigment. They will be totally without colour and are popularly known as 'snow corns'. Statistically, only one in every 16 offspring will be of this type (but of course, once one has been produced, the proportion can be increased by arranging other, more efficient, mating combinations).

Note that anerythristic snakes are notated rrBB (i.e. normal black but no red) and amelanistic snakes are notated RRbb (i.e. normal red but no black). Therefore anerythristic snakes can only produce one type of gamete: 'rB', and amelanistic snakes can only produce one type of gamete: 'Rb'.

By adding these together, i.e. one set of genes from the male and another set from the female, it can be seen that all offspring from this cross will carry the genes 'RrBb', i.e. double heterozygous.

If these double heterozygous offspring are crossed with each other the situation becomes rather complicated! Both the male and the

female can produce four possible types of gamete – the R can be accompanied by B or b, and the r can also be accompanied by B or b, producing: RB, Rb, rB or rb.

By combining these possibilities using a grid matrix, we get the following result, using a hypothetical, statistically perfect clutch of 16 young:

	RB	Rb	rB	rb
RB	RRBB	RRBb	RrBB	RrBb
Rb	RRBb	RRbb	RrBb	Rrbb
rB	RrBB	RrBb	rrBB	rrBb
rb	RrBb	Rrbb	rrBb	rrbb

There are therefore nine different genetic types present:

1	wild-type, normal (RRBB)	
2	wild-type, heterozygous for black (RRBb)	
2	wild-type, heterozygous for red (RrBB)	normal markings
4	wild-type, heterozygous for both, (RrBb)*	
1	no black, normal red (RRbb)	
2	no black, heterozygous for red (Rrbb)	amelanistic
1	no red, normal black (rrBB)	
2	no red, heterozygous for black (rrBb)	anerythristic
1	no black or red	snow corn

The ratios of the *apparent* types, as opposed to genetic types, are therefore as follows: 9 wild-type: 3 amelanistic: 3 anerythristic: 1 snow corn.

(* These four snakes, RrBb, are genetically identical to the parents.)

(**See colour photographs on page 119.**)

SELLING

This section is concerned with the selling of surplus stock, usually as a result of successfully breeding a pair of snakes. The advice given under BUYING should be read also, in order to see what a customer will expect of the breeder he or she is buying from. Most private individuals sell their snakes through a society, to friends or to a local pet dealer. The important points about selling are that the breeder has a moral obligation to sex the snakes correctly, to give appropriate advice on their care, and to give details of the parents, i.e. whether the parents are related or not, which subspecies or strain they belong to and so on. It will be easier to sell hatchling snakes if they are feeding and most purchasers, especially if they are relatively inexperienced, will require some assurance that this is the case, especially with species which are known to be sometimes difficult to start.

Prices of snakes vary enormously according to the quality of the stock, as well as to supply and demand. Many formerly rare species have dropped in price in recent years because the numbers of people breeding them have risen, but there should still be few problems in disposing of well-marked healthy hatchlings at a price which is fair to both parties.

If snakes cannot be collected personally by the purchaser they must be sent by road, rail or air. It is illegal to send snakes through the mail in Europe, the United States and probably elsewhere. Whichever method of transport is used, check that the carrier has no regulations restricting the carriage of livestock in general, and snakes in particular. Boxes containing snakes for shipment should be strongly made, of plywood or polystyrene, and each snake should be packed separately in a ventillated plastic tub or a cotton bag. The tubs or bags containing the snakes should be placed in the centre of the box, surrounded by packing/insulation material such as polystyrene beads or crumpled newspaper. The box must be labelled 'livestock' and the name, address and telephone number of the recipient should be prominently displayed. It is also a good idea to display the sender's name and address in case of difficulties in delivering the package. Arrangements must be made with the purchaser to ensure that he or she will be able to collect the snakes as soon as they arrive at his or her home, local railway station or airport, and he or she should be advised of their estimated time of arrival. The sender should also check that the snakes have, in fact, arrived at their destination.

SEX DETERMINATION

If breeding is to be attempted, it is obviously important to be able to tell the difference between male and female snakes. Not only will this be necessary in order to put together a pair in the first place, but any resulting offspring will usually need to be sexed before they are disposed of. Few snakes show any external differences between the sexes, and males and females can only be identified by examining their reproductive organs. Males have paired hemipenes which are normally inverted (turned inside out) and lie along the base of the tail. When mating takes place, one or other of these hemipenes is everted (pushed out), through the cloacal opening, and used in copulation. Sex determination therefore consists of examining

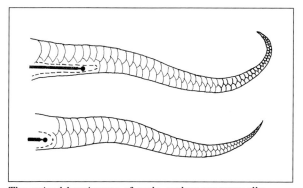

The paired hemipenes of male snakes are normally inverted, and lie at the base of the tail. They can be detected by gently inserting a metal probe. Females have a much shorter chamber, containing the musk glands

the snake for the presence of hemipenes. There are three common ways in which this can be done.

1 Scale count/tail length/spurs

Because they house the hemipenes, the tails of male snakes are normally relatively longer than those of females of the same species and subspecies. This, in turn, causes them to have a greater number of scales beneath the tail (the sub-caudals). The sexes can therefore be told apart by comparing the tail lengths of similarly sized individuals and/or counting the sub-caudal scales. Scale counts are best carried out on shed skins rather than live snakes. Unfortunately, this method is not totally reliable because males and females show some variation. Thus, long-tailed females may have longer tails than short-tailed males, even when the average tail length among the population is substantially greater in males.

Boas and pythons can sometimes be sexed superficially by examining their spurs. These can be found on either side of the cloaca and are used by males during courtship. The spurs

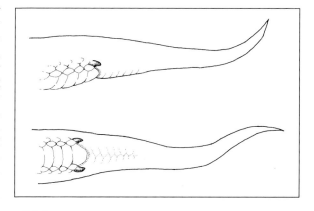

Pythons and boas can sometimes be sexed by looking at the spurs at the base of the tail: those of males are larger

Sand and Shovel-nosed Snakes

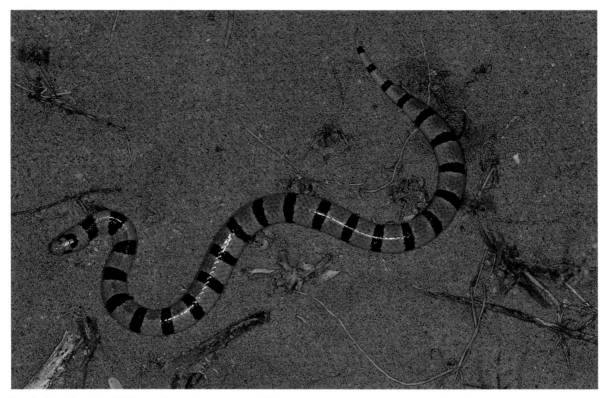

Banded sand snake, *Chilomeniscus cinctus*, a small insectivorous species from a desert habitat

Sonoran shovel-nosed snake, *Chionactis palarostris*

Sunbeam Snake and the Mexican Python

The Mexican dwarf python, *Loxocemus unicolor*, is the only New World python, and is a burrowing species

Scales of the sunbeam snake, *Xenopeltis bicolor*, a burrowing snake from South-East Asia

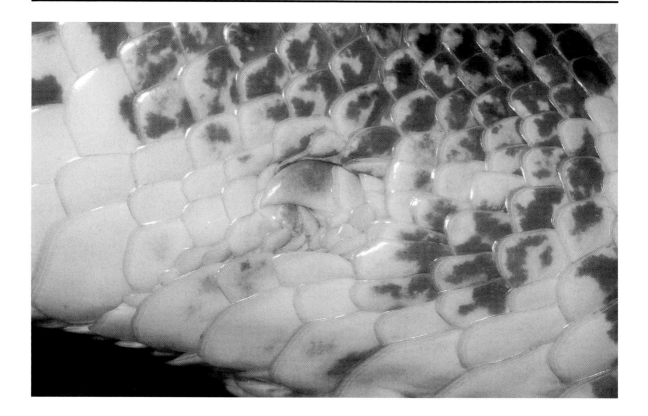

of males are longer than those of females, which are sometimes absent altogether, or so small as to be virtually invisible. As with comparing tail lengths, this method is quick and easy, but is not 100 per cent reliable.

Male pythons and boas both have prominent spurs found at the base of the tail; this feature can sometimes be used to sex the snakes

2 Probing

Probing is a very reliable way of identifying the sexes, but must be carried out with great care if injuries to the snake are to be avoided. The best instrument to use is a purpose-made snake probe, which should be of stainless surgical steel, polished and with a rounded tip. A set of different-sized probes will be required if a variety of snakes of different ages are to be checked.

Firstly, the tip of the appropriate probe should be smeared with a small quantity of petroleum jelly or antiseptic cream in order to lubricate it. The snake is then held at the base of the tail and the body allowed to hang downwards slightly (although it should be supported, either by allowing it to rest on a table or by being held by an assistant). The probe is now gently inserted into the cloaca, a little to one side of the centre line, and pushed back towards the tip of the tail. It may be helpful to twirl the probe slightly between the thumb and fingers as this operation is carried out. If hemipenes are present, the probe will pass back along one of them to a distance equivalent to about six or more sub-caudal scales. Females have a short musk gland which

opens in roughly the same position as the hemipenes but this is much shallower, usually reaching to only two or three sub-caudals. If the probe will not easily enter on one side of the cloaca it should be withdrawn and tried on the other side of the centre-line. Whatever happens, *do not force the probe*.

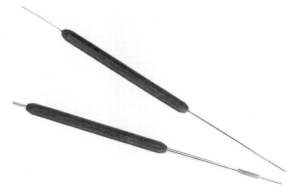

Sexing probes are available in a variety of sizes, for sexing anything from a hatchling kingsnake to an adult python. They are not difficult to use but great care must be taken to ensure that the snake is firmly restrained before the probe is inserted

Probing in progress: the probe is gently inserted into
the cloaca and eased back into one of the cavities at
the base of the tail. If it passes more than two or three
sub-caudal scales, as here, the snake is a male. (The
arrow indicates the position of the tip of the probe)

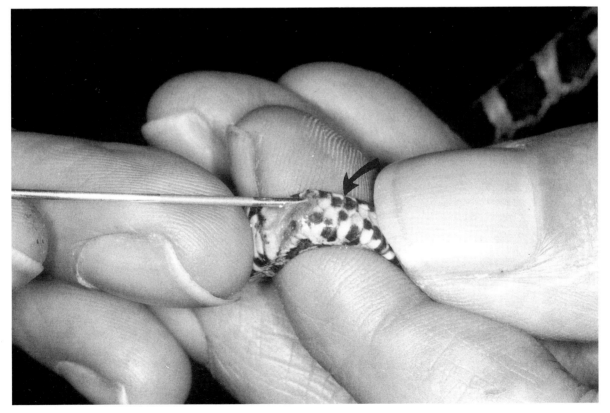

With females, the probe can only be inserted to the
depth of two or three sub-caudal scales

Water Snakes

Dice snake, *Natrix tessellata*, a semi-aquatic European species which does fairly well in captivity

Mangrove water snake, *Nerodia fasciata compressicauda*, red phase

Venomous Snakes

Hairy bush viper, *Atheris hispida*. Many venomous snakes are attractive, but they are totally unsuitable for most private collections

Everting the hemipenes of a young snake, known as 'popping'. By applying gentle pressure at the base of the tail, the hemipenes can be made to pop out. The technique becomes more difficult as the snake grows and can rarely be made to work with adults

3 Everting the hemipenes

In some cases, the hemipenes can be everted or 'popped' by putting pressure on the base of the tail with the thumb and gently pushing upwards with a rolling motion. This technique works better with hatchling and juvenile snakes than with adults, which are more muscular, and requires some practice. If the hemipenes pop out then, obviously, the snake is a male, but if they do not then this could be due to an incorrect technique. If in doubt, probe all 'females' after attempting to pop them.

Once the snakes have been sexed conclusively, by whichever method is employed, it is useful to identify them by noting small differences which are usually present in their markings. This avoids the necessity of carrying out repeated manipulations with the same animals.

SEX RATIOS

Some reptiles, such as turtles and some lizards, have temperature-dependent sex determination (in other words, the sex of the offspring can be controlled by the temperature at which the eggs are incubated), but this does not apply to snakes, in which the sex is determined genetically (as in humans) and which normally display a 50:50 sex ratio (on average). Although the sex of even hatchling snakes can usually be determined accurately by following the instructions under SEX DETERMINATION, this may not always be possible. The only alternative is to obtain a group of animals which will, with luck, contain at least one member of each sex. But how big a group? The laws of probability can be used to calculate the chance of obtaining any combination of males and females in a given sample, using a simple statistical formula. The following table gives the chances of obtaining various numbers of pairs from samples ranging from two to ten, assuming a normal 50:50 sex ratio within the population. It is clear that the more animals there are initially, the better the chances of obtaining one or more pairs. However, the chances do not get better in direct proportion to the number in the sample, and above a certain size of sample the chance only increases marginally.

It should be realised, however, that even where there is a 50:50 sex ratio among the population, this value may not occur in wild-caught animals. In certain species, males are more active than females at particular times of the year, notably spring, and are therefore more likely to be captured, especially if the method of hunting them is selective, for instance road-hunting at night. Thus, some batches of snakes will contain nearly all males, and it is always best to attempt to sex snakes using one of the methods described rather than relying on the law of averages.

Statistical Probability of Obtaining Pairs

Sample	Expected number of pairs					
	0	**1**	**2**	**3**	**4**	**5**
2	50.0	50.0				
3	25.0	75.0				
4	12.5	50.0	37.5			
5	6.25	31.25	62.5			
6	3.125	18.75	46.875	31.25		
7	1.526	10.937	32.812	54.687		
8	0.781	6.25	21.875	39.307	27.344	
9	0.391	3.516	14.062	31.812	49.219	
10	0.195	1.953	8.789	23.437	41.016	24.609

The figures show the *percentage chance* of obtaining the numbers of pairs from the total number of animals in the sample. For instance, out of seven animals the chances of obtaining three pairs (i.e. three of one sex and four of the other) are just over 54 per cent, and out of ten animals the chances of not getting any pairs at all would be 0.0195 per cent – almost two in a thousand – while the chances of an even split (five males and five females) would be 24.609 per cent.

Note that the chance of not getting any pairs at all never disappears altogether, however many animals are in the initial sample, but, for all practical purposes, a group of 5 animals is highly likely (100 per cent – 6.25 per cent = 93.75 per cent probability) to contain at least one pair and a sample of four only slightly less likely (100 per cent – 12.5 per cent = 87.5 per cent) to contain one or two pairs.

SHOVEL-NOSED SNAKES

Shovel-nosed snakes are found in the south-western corner of North America, where they inhabit arid sandy or stony desert habitats. Their adaptations to a subterranean lifestyle include smooth shiny scales and a flattened head. They are small, usually less than 30 cm (1 ft) in total length, and feed on invertebrates such as scorpions, spiders, crickets and the larvae of beetles, etc. Two species are recognised. Both are cream or yellow in colour, with a series of black bands across the back. Some have additional secondary bands which may be red or black, according to species and subspecies. Four subspecies of the western shovel-nose are recognised, and two of the Sonoran shovel-nose.

Chionactis occipitalis, the western shovel-nosed snake
- ☐ *C. o. annulata*, Colorado Desert shovel-nosed snake
- ☐ *C. o. klauberi*, Tucson shovel-nosed snake
- ☐ *C. o. occipitalis*, Mojave shovel-nosed snake
- ☐ *C. o. talpina*, Nevada shovel-nosed snake

Chionactis palarostris, the Sonoran shovel-nosed snake **(In colour on page 122.)**
- ☐ *C. p. organica*, the Organ Pipe shovel-nosed snake, is found in extreme south-western Arizona, mostly within the Organ Pipe Cactus National Monument, and in adjacent parts of Sonora, Mexico.
- ☐ *C. p. palarostris* is restricted to Mexico.

C. palarostris is the more colourful of the two, and has broad red saddles between the black bands. *C. occipitalis* has smaller red saddles, although, in some populations, e.g. *C. o. occipitalis* from the Mojave desert, these are absent altogether. Because they are similar in habits, and superficially resemble one another, both are dealt with together.

They are desert snakes whose habitat includes pockets of sand, such as are found in dry river washes and gravelly and rocky desert – typical 'cactus country'. Both species are a pleasure to keep in captivity. They require an inch or two of sand in which to live and a diet of crickets, waxworm larvae, etc. (A small proportion seem reluctant to eat crickets and soon become thin – in this case, alternative food should be tried until an acceptable diet is established.) Despite their desert origins, they require drinking water at all times, otherwise they will soon dehydrate. Some individuals seem to prefer to drink from the side of the vivarium, etc. after it has been sprayed. A temperature of around 25-30°C (77-86°F)

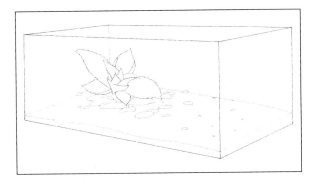

A shallow cage, with a few inches of free-running sand on the bottom and perhaps a few stones and succulent plants for interest, makes an attractive and practical set-up for shovel-nosed snakes and similar small desert species

SKIN-SHEDDING

As snakes grow, they shed the outer layer of their skin at regular intervals. The scientific term for this is 'ecdysis'. Young snakes tend to slough more frequently than older individuals, whose growth rate will have slowed right down. The sequence of events starts with the secretion of an oily substance between the old, uppermost layer of skin and the new skin which is lying beneath it. This causes the snake to appear bluish or dull. The eyes look opaque (because they, too, are covered with a scale which will come away with the rest of the skin). After four or five days the eyes will clear and the skin will look fairly normal again and shedding, or sloughing, will occur four to seven

appears to suit them, although a gradient, as provided by a heat tape or heat pad, is recommended. They are relatively easily sexed by probing, and breeding should be possible. The only foreseeable problem would be the provision of a damp substrate in which the eggs could be laid.

These snakes lend themselves to a naturalistic set-up in which rocks, cactus skeletons and living succulent plants can add to the aesthetic appeal. In addition, they may be kept (with caution) with other desert reptiles, such as banded geckos (*Coleonyx*), since they appear to show no tendency to eat vertebrate prey unless this is very much smaller than themselves. Owing to their burrowing habits, they are not always visible, although their period of activity usually begins in the evening regardless of whether the vivarium is lit or not.

C. palarostris is undoubtedly the most attractive species, but also the most difficult to obtain. It is protected throughout its range by virtue of the fact that this falls mostly within Mexico or the Organ Pipe Cactus National Monument. However, all forms are attractive and interesting, and the fact that their natural history, especially with respect to breeding, is little known, should add to their appeal.

Prior to shedding, an oil is secreted between the old and new layers of skin, making the markings dull and the eyes milky, as in this juvenile Baird's ratsnake, *Elaphe bairdi*

days after this. The process starts with the snake freeing the skin around its upper and lower jaws, often by rubbing its snout on some rough object. The outer skin is then peeled back and the snake crawls out of it, leaving the discarded skin inside out, and its new skin bright and shiny.

Problems with shedding rarely occur with healthy snakes. However, if the snake goes dull and then fails to shed, the skin may become wrinkled and dry and will not come away easily. The remedy for this is to soak the snake, either by placing it in a tub containing a small amount of water and leaving this in a warm place (making sure that the lid is on securely), or by placing it in a cotton bag (e.g. a pillow case) which has been half-filled with damp sphagnum moss. If the problem repeats itself every time the snake comes up for a slough, then it is likely that conditions are wrong. Often it will be found that the snake is reluctant to soak itself, possibly because its water bowl is placed in an exposed position. The use of a partially covered water bowl, as described under the heading CAGE FURNISHINGS, will often correct this. A small number of species, mainly from tropical rain forests, require a higher humidity than the general run of snakes and it may be necessary to spray these snakes occasionally to increase the humidity, especially just before they are due to shed. Persistent failure to shed properly may be due to a disease or hormone imbalance in the snake. Usually other symptoms will also be present and the

Shedding commences at the snout, and the snake then crawls out of the skin, leaving it inside out

remedy should be sought through the services of a vet.

Another problem which can arise occasionally is failure to shed the scales covering the eyes, even though the rest of the skin comes away completely – if the scale is not removed then the problem will increase with subsequent sheddings. With large snakes, the easiest way to remove this scale is to grasp the snake firmly behind the head with one hand and use a finger nail from the other hand to lift the scale. This can be quite difficult as the edge of the scale is often covered by surrounding (ocular) scales and the eye may have to be 'rolled' slightly to gain access. With smaller snakes, an alternative method is to wrap a piece of adhesive tape around a finger with the gummed side outwards. Repeatedly pressing this onto the eye will often dislodge the scale.

STRESS

Stress is the single most common cause of death in snakes. Unfortunately, it is difficult to define stress with any degree of accuracy, but it includes all those effects brought about by a change in environment, overcrowding, lack of food or water and unsympathetic handling. These problems combine to lead to a refusal to feed and lowered resistance to disease (which, in turn, produces more stress). It is not possible to look at a snake and decide immediately if it is suffering from stress, nor can the results always be predicted. Sometimes, correcting the environment can bring about an immediate and dramatic return to normal, but at other times even sophisticated medication and the very best attention fail to reverse the situation and the eventual result is the death of the snake.

Snakes which are fit and healthy are far more tolerant of variation in temperature, humidity, frequency of feeding and handling. Nervous snakes which are underweight or suffering from a low-level parasite or bacterial infection, will decline quickly if any of the above details deviate greatly from their preferred range. It follows that newly acquired snakes, especially if they are wild-caught, should be given first-class conditions and extra attention so that anything amiss can be corrected before it is too

T

late. Look out for abnormal behaviour for the species (constant prowling around the cage for secretive species, lack of activity for more active diurnal species), and for refusal to feed, poor shedding and dull coloration.

Bringing a stressed snake back to normal can be a very long-term project. It must be given seclusion, especially when offered food, and handled as little as possible. Snakes which become thin quickly and have dry skin are often dehydrated. Some species and individuals have problems finding a water bowl if they are under stress and they should be given a partially covered bowl (see CAGES) or sprayed regularly. In extreme cases it may be necessary to place them in a container of water and leave the lid on overnight so that they are forcibly exposed to high humidity.

Certain species are more inclined to suffer from stress than others. Very active species will not feel comfortable in small containers, and secretive species will feel equally unhappy if placed in a large open cage with nowhere to hide. Therefore, it follows that some knowledge of the snake's natural history will be necessary. In general, avoid large active species: it is almost impossible to provide accommodation which will satisfy them. Instead, buy captive-bred hatchlings wherever possible, since these are far more likely to adapt well.

SUNBEAM SNAKE (In colour on page 123.)

The sunbeam snake, *Xenopeltis unicolor*, is a strange South-East Asian species which is occasionally available. It grows to about 1 m (3 ft) in length and is dark grey on top with a pearly white underside. Its most remarkable characteristic, and the reason for its common name, is the high degree of iridescence over the whole of its head and body. Its head is flattened, and it spends most of its time beneath the ground.

In captivity, this species has a bad reputation because it is often imported in poor condition and fails to thrive. However, healthy individuals make beautiful captives as they are easy to handle and feed very well on mice. Unfortunately, captive breeding has not yet been achieved.

THERMOREGULATION

Snakes, like all reptiles, are ecto-therms. This means that they cannot produce their own heat (as we can) but must rely on outside sources to supply it. Fish are also ecto-therms, which is why tropical species have to be kept in warm water. Similarly, tropical reptiles also need a reliable heat source, but there are some important differences in the way the two groups regulate their body temperatures. Fish live in an aquatic environment and therefore have little opportunity to control their temperatures – the water acts as a heat-sink and any attempt they made to raise their body temperatures would soon be lost to the environment. In other words, they 'make do' with the temperature of the water in which they live and each species has evolved to suit its particular environment. The scientific name for this is 'passive thermoregulation'.

Some snakes, such as those which live their entire lives burrowed into the soil, are also passive thermoregulators, but most species, including almost all of those which are kept in captivity, are able to exert some control over their body temperature by using a number of 'tricks', some of which are to do with their physiology and some of which are behavioural. In other words, they are able to maintain a more stable temperature by moving from warm to cool areas and vice versa. These species are known as 'active thermoregulators'. In the wild, they can obtain their heat in two ways: radiation (i.e. from the sun), or conduction (i.e. from the substrate on or in which they live).

Whether they obtain their heat through radiation or conduction, there are several other implications of snakes' thermoregulation which concern their care in captivity and it is important to understand exactly what these are before they can be kept successfully. In nature, they warm up and cool down according to the time of day and also according to the season – they have a daily and seasonal thermal rhythm. Because each species has evolved in such a way as to fit in with this rhythm, its body is geared up to it. It is not 'kind' to keep reptiles constantly warm, day and night, summer and winter: they need to be allowed to cool down and warm up. In fact, most species have built-in biological clocks which control their activities. If they are not allowed to behave naturally they will not remain in good condition and, in particular, they will not breed.

Desert habitat of numerous snakes and lizards in California. A wide range of temperatures is available to the reptile inhabitants as they move from sunlight to shade, or retreat into burrows. In this way they can control their body temperatures to within narrow limits

Breeding cycles are especially dependent on thermal rhythms. Most species mate in the spring, when the days are getting longer and warmer, and the females lay their eggs or give birth during the summer, so that the young have the best possible chance of finding plenty of food before winter. During the winter, many species are preparing themselves for reproduction by manufacturing egg or sperm cells – if they do not experience a cool period, this will not occur and they will be sterile. Even in the tropics, where there may not be a recognisable winter, there will almost certainly be a cooler time of the year (usually the rainy season) which reptiles are tuned into. (For more information see under HIBERNATION.)

Daily temperature cycles

How can allowances be made for daily temperature rhythms in captivity? Fortunately, due to the built-in biological clocks mentioned above, the animals will control their own rhythms, provided that they are allowed to. This means giving them a range of temperatures to choose from. Most species are most active at around 25-30°C (77-86°F), although there is some variation. By creating a suitable thermal gradient, we can be sure that they will be able to find the part of the cage which suits them best at any given time. This can be done by positioning the heater so that it heats *one end of the cage only*. By moving from one end of the cage to the other, the animal can control its own temperature. Furthermore, there is no need to boost the heat at night. If the average temperature of the cage drops, so much the better: the animal's body will 'expect' this to happen. For exactly this reason, the fitting of a thermostat into the heating circuit is superfluous, and may even be harmful (unless it is set very high or very low in order to guard against severe under- or overheating).

Species which obtain their heat by basking (very few, in fact) should be given an overhead heat source such as a spotlight, but this should also be directed at one end of the cage. The spotlight should be turned off at night, and, if necessary, background heat supplied by means of a bottom heater, as described above.

Whichever method is used, it is important to make sure that other aspects of the cage layout do not interfere with the animal's choice of position: for instance, if it is secretive, it should have a hiding place at both the warm end and the cool end.

The ideal temperature ranges for various species differ somewhat according to their origins, and there will always be some variation. However, the animal's behaviour will always be the best indication of its requirements. If it spends all of its time at the cool end of the cage, the heat source should be turned down slightly; if it spends all of its time at the warm end, it should be increased, perhaps by using more powerful equipment. Ideally, the animal should be found to shuttle from one part of the cage to the other throughout the day, although snakes which have recently fed will normally spend more time at the warm end, since the higher temperatures aid digestion. Similarly, snakes which are about to shed their skin or lay eggs will also tend to spend more time than usual at the warmer end of the cage. For information on the equipment and methods of providing heating to captive snakes, see HEATING.

TIGER RATSNAKE

The tiger ratsnake, *Spilotes pullatus*, is a large South American colubrid with only a distant relationship to the true ratsnakes (genus *Elaphe*). This species is a slender black or brown snake with varying amounts of yellow or white markings on the head and neck. It grows to well over 2 m (6½ ft) and can be aggressive and irascible. Handling a large specimen is not for the faint-hearted!

They can do quite well in captivity if they overcome the initial stress caused by their capture and subsequent transportation, but they often carry large parasite burdens – on no account should newly acquired individuals be housed near established snakes (see QUARANTINE). Unfortunately, they rarely tame down sufficiently to warrant the effort and risks involved in settling them in.

VENOMOUS SNAKES

Two families of snakes contain only venomous snakes: the Elapidae, or cobras, and the Viperidae, or vipers (including pit vipers such as rattlesnakes). In addition, a small proportion of typical snakes, Colubridae, produce venom which is delivered via their rear fangs. Some of these, such as the boomslang and the mangrove snake, are also potentially dangerous to humans.

The keeping of any of these species should only be undertaken by very experienced snake-keepers, and then only after long and serious consideration. Apart from the very obvious dangers to the keeper (and possibly his or her family and neighbours), there are several legal and moral obligations to be taken into account, including the possession of a dangerous wild animals licence (in the UK), exemption from local restrictions on the keeping of dangerous snakes (in most parts of the USA) and the necessity to maintain a stock of the appropriate anti-venin (see LAW).

Aside from these considerations, the care and breeding of venomous snakes follows much the same pattern as other species from corresponding parts of the world. Plenty of venomous snakes are rodent-eaters, and many adapt well to captivity. A number of the more attractive and interesting species are bred in reasonably large numbers although, obviously, the demand for them is limited. Popular species include several of the smaller rattlesnakes, (*Crotalus* and *Sistrurus* species), palm vipers (*Bothrops* species), bush vipers (*Atheris* species) **(in colour on page 127)**, true vipers (*Vipera* species) and African vipers (*Bitis* species). A number of these genera contain species which have fairly mild venom, but injuries are always unpleasant, to say the least. Members of the cobra family are less frequently seen in captivity because they are more difficult to handle safely.

In general, members of the cobra family lay eggs, whereas the vipers give birth to living young, but there are exceptions in both familes.

There will be no attempt here to give further details since venomous snakes are of interest only to a few specialists. The purpose of this note is simply to point out that the maintenance of venomous snakes does not differ fundamentally from that of other snakes, except in the important aspect of security. With dozens of species of non-venomous snakes to choose from, it is difficult to understand why private individuals would wish to endanger themselves by keeping dangerously venomous snakes.

Banded rock rattlesnake, *Crotalus lepidus klauberi*. All species of rattler are venomous and cannot therefore be kept in most countries without a special licence

A few species of rear-fanged colubrids are considered to be dangerous in some countries and can only be kept after a special licence has been obtained. The long-nosed tree snake, *Dryophis nasuta*, is one example

WATER SNAKES

The term 'water snake' is used to label a number of unrelated groups of snakes from various parts of the world. Of those which may be available from dealers, three groups may be recognised:

- [ ] *Enhydris* species from Asia
- [ ] *Natrix* species from Asia and Europe
- [ ] *Nerodia* species from North America

Their care is somewhat different and so they are dealt with separately.

Enhydris species

The Asian *Enhydris*, of which a number of species are recognised, are highly aquatic snakes which are rarely found out of water except during heavy rain, when the surrounding countryside is flooded. Most are small brown snakes with smooth shiny scales. In captivity, they can be treated more or less as tropical fish: kept in an aquarium containing several inches of water and heated by a submersible aquarium heater set at approximately 27°C (80°F). A dry platform should be available, however, so that they can crawl out, and this may be overhung with a spotlight, giving them an opportunity to bask – some seem to take advantage of this facility, while others rarely, if ever, venture out of the water. They feed on fish and tadpoles, and guppies form a cheap and reliable food source.

In common with many other Asian snakes, these little water snakes are often in poor shape when they arrive and are difficult to keep alive. Apart from the usual variety of reptilian parasites and diseases, animals under stress may become troubled with a fungal infection in which patches of grey form on the scales. If they survive their initial vulnerability, *Enhydris* make good and interesting captives. The females give birth to small litters of live young, which wrap their tails around aquatic plants and hang motionless in the water waiting for an appropriately sized fish to swim by. A few colonies have continued to produce young regularly, but there is little information on their breeding requirements.

Natrix species (In colour on page 126.)

The genus *Natrix* is widespread and includes three European species as well as numerous Asian members. The status of several of the latter is in some doubt. Generally speaking, these water snakes are only semi-aquatic, and can be kept in a similar manner to garter snakes (see GARTER SNAKES). However, they are not nearly so successful as captives, and many require a diet which includes at least some amphibians. Of the European species, *N. tessellata* is probably the best, with *N. natrix* the least satisfactory. *N. maura* appears to do quite well, but is rarely kept. The Asian species are plagued by a poor record due to their state of health on importation. In addition, several of the so-called 'water snakes' from Asia are rear-fanged species and, although probably not dangerous, are best avoided by the non-specialist.

Nerodia species (In colour on page 126.)

American 'water' snakes are now placed in the genus *Nerodia*, having formerly been included in *Natrix*. An additional small grouping has been renamed *Regina*, but these are of little interest to snake-keepers because they eat mainly crayfish and other crustaceans. Of the more familiar *Nerodia* species, the various forms of *N. sipedon*, *N. erythrogaster* and *N. cyclopion* fare well in captivity. Although they have a reputation for bad tempers, young or half-grown individuals settle down quite quickly. They are active snakes and require fairly large cages, which should be kept *dry*. Failure to do this will result in sores and blisters between the ventral scales, and this can lead to fatal results. The ideal arrangement is for a large, partially covered water bowl to be placed in the cage so that the snakes can soak

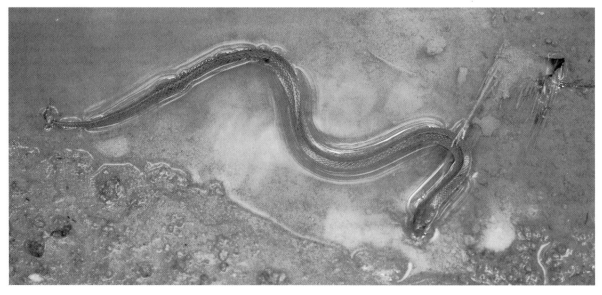

The European grass snake, *Natrix natrix*, does not make an especially good captive unless kept in an outside enclosure

occasionally. If they are fed on live fish, these can be added to the bowl. Most individuals, however, are willing to accept dead fish and this makes their maintenance more convenient. The remarks on feeding fish to snakes should be carefully read (see the special note under FEEDING). As with all fish-eating snakes,

Members of the genus *Enhydris* are amongst the most aquatic of all colubrid snakes. This Malaysian example is probably *E. fordi*

Nerodia cages soon become dirty and smelly, so they require regular cleaning. These snakes also require feeding more often than rodent-eating species since fish are not as nutritious, but some water snakes will learn to eat dead rodents, especially if these are first scented with some fish slime before being placed in the cage.

A temperature of about 25°C (77°F), with a thermal gradient, is satisfactory. If it is intended to breed them, a temperature drop during the winter will probably be necessary. Unfortunately, there is little interest in breeding these species since they are easily obtainable from the wild and the demand is small.

Magazines and Journals

Few publications cater exclusively for the snake-keeper. There are, however, herpetological societies in most parts of the world and several of these publish journals and newsletters that contain material that may be of interest. Other journals are mainly scientifically orientated and are principally of interest to those snake-keepers with academic leanings.

Publications marked with an asterisk regularly contain advertisements placed by snake-breeders wishing to sell surplus stock.

Europe

*British Journal of Herpetology, Bulletin of the British Herpetological Society** Both published by the British Herpetological Society, London. The latter often contains articles and notes relating to reptiles in captivity.

Herpetofauna A well-produced colour magazine with many articles relating to the care of reptiles. Published by Herpetofauna Verlags, Federal Republic of Germany (in German).

The Herptile Amateur-orientated quarterly journal of the International Herpetological Society, England.

Lacerta The monthly journal of the Nederlandse Vereniging voor Herpetologie en Terrariumkunde, the Netherlands (in Dutch).

*Litteratura Serpentium** Quarterly journal of the Dutch Snake Society, published in Dutch and English editions.

Salamandra Journal of the Deutschen Gesellschaft für Herpetologie und Terrarienkunde, Federal Republic of Germany (in German).

*The Snake-breeder** Monthly magazine produced by Snake Keeper Publications, England.

North America

Copeia Scientific journal published by the American Society of Ichthyologists and Herpetologists, Florida.

Herpetologica Scientific journal published by the Herpetolgists' League, Lawrence, Kansas.

Journal of Herpetology, Herpetological Review Both published by the Society for the Study of Amphibians and Reptiles, Ohio.

*The Vivarium** A beautifully produced colour magazine/journal published by the American Federation of Herpetoculturists. Available by subscription or through local distributors in the United States and Europe.

Australasia

Herpetofauna Published by the Australasian Affiliation of Herpetological Societies, Sydney, Australia.

Africa

Journal of the Herpetological Society of Africa Published by the Herpetological Society of Africa, South Africa.

In addition to the publications listed, many journals and newsletters are produced by regional herpetological societies, especially in the United States and Britain. These publications may be of local interest only, but often contain articles and observations of more general interest. In addition, many carry advertisements for captive-bred snakes. It is not feasible to list them but details are usually available from local zoos, museums or libraries.

INDEX
BY LATIN NAME

INDEX
BY COMMON NAME

A–Z of Snake Keeping

■ ■ ■

Chris Mattison

with photographs by the author

No wonder the keeping of snakes in private collections is such a fast-growing hobby. As this color-filled guide demonstrates, many species of snake thrive in captivity, and breed readily away from the wild.

For anyone interested in this challenging and fascinating hobby, *A–Z of Snake Keeping* is essential reading. Dozens of species are treated in A–Z form, from Albinos and Boas to Water Snakes and Vipers. All aspects of the care and keeping of snakes get careful coverage in an easy-reference, fully illustrated format, including cages, heating, feeding, and hygiene. Vital tips help the beginning keeper learn how to choose a species for keeping, how to buy healthy specimens, how to maintain the optimum environment, what is normal behavior for each species, and what to do when a snake becomes ill.

No longer is snake keeping an exotic hobby. The endangered-species breeding programs at zoos and other research centers are turning up a wealth of information that makes it possible for a wide range of nature lovers to care for one of earth's oldest and hardiest forms of life.